MathsWise

BOOK 3

RAY ALLAN
HENRY COMPTON SCHOOL, FULHAM, LONDON

MARTIN WILLIAMS
GEORGE MITCHELL SCHOOL, LEYTON, LONDON

OXFORD
UNIVERSITY PRESS

OXFORD
UNIVERSITY PRESS

Great Clarendon Street, Oxford OX2 6DP

Oxford University Press is a department of the University of Oxford.
It furthers the University's objective of excellence in research, scholarship, and
education by publishing worldwide in

Oxford   New York

Auckland   Cape Town   Dar es Salaam   Hong Kong   Karachi
Kuala Lumpur   Madrid   Melbourne   Mexico City   Nairobi
New Delhi   Shanghai   Taipei   Toronto

With offices in

Argentina   Austria   Brazil   Chile   Czech Republic   France   Greece
Guatemala   Hungary   Italy   Japan   Poland   Portugal   Singapore
South Korea   Switzerland   Thailand   Turkey   Ukraine   Vietnam

Oxford is a registered trade mark of Oxford University Press
in the UK and in certain other countries

First published 2001

10   9   8   7

British Library Cataloguing in Publication Data

Data available

ISBN-13: 978 0 19 914776 2

ISBN-10: 0-19-914776-0

Typeset by TechSet Ltd. Gateshead, Tyne and Wear.
Printed in Hong Kong

About This Book

Mathswise Book 3 is the third in a series of three books spanning levels 1 – 4 of the National Curriculum in England and Wales. It is aimed at students in year 9.

It has been written to give you plenty of practice at the basic concepts in mathematics so you can build up confidence and achieve your best level in the Key Stage 3 tests at the end of year 9.

The authors have many years teaching experience at this level and all the activities and exercises in this book are built on their considerable knowledge of what students in year 9 are able to understand.

Each unit in the book starts with the **learning outcomes** of the unit so that you can see what you are expected to learn.

There is a box highlighting key mathematical words

Examples are often given to show you how to approach questions. They are in blue shaded boxes, for example:

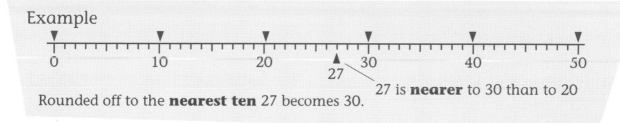

Example

Rounded off to the **nearest ten** 27 becomes 30.

27 is **nearer** to 30 than to 20

This icon highlights Numeracy focus pages. These pages encourage numeracy practice in other contexts.

There are regular **revision exercises** throughout the book. Make sure you can do the revision questions before you move on to the next unit.

Towards the end of the book there are three sections called **Street Maths**. These sections allow you to practise all the skills you have learnt in the book.

The **answers** to the exercises in the book are available in a separate book from the publishers. See the back cover for details.

CONTENTS

1 THINKING SKILLS

This work is about the methods and thinking skills that you use to get a correct answer. Concentrate on how to solve problems as well as getting the right answer. Talk with your friends and your teacher about problem solving. Make your own notes about what you do.

TASK 1 Farmer Benjamin decides to give away a square field.
He gives $\frac{1}{4}$ of the field to the Church.
He tells his four sons that they must share the rest of the field between them, in four equal shares.

Draw a square, like the one here.
Work out how the brothers will make four equal shares out of the remaining land.

The conditions of the gift:
- The church cannot change the shape or area of its land.
- The brothers must share the remaining land equally – each plot must have the same area and the same shape.

Church land

TASK 2 These clocks show the times in:
Dublin, London, New York, Rio de Janeiro, Paris, Moscow and Cairo.
Read the clues below to decide in which city each clock is situated.

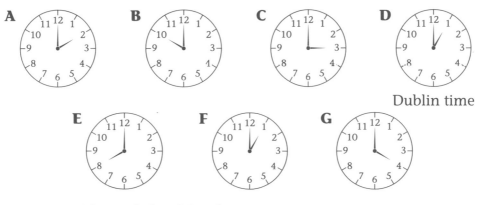

Dublin time

- Rio de Janeiro is 3 hours behind London.
- Rio de Janeiro is 2 hours in front of New York.
- Moscow is 2 hours ahead of Paris.
- The London and Dublin clocks show the same time.
- When it is 4 p.m. in Cairo, it is 2 p.m. in London.
- When the London clock shows 11 a.m., the Paris clock will show 12 p.m.

TASK 3 Work out what each symbol is worth.

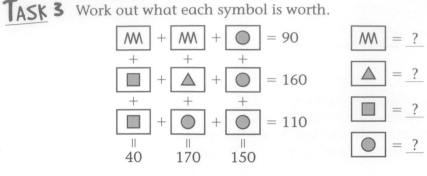

TASK 4
Copy the number grid shown below.
Read each question and each answer.
Cross out the numbers as you work through the questions and answers.
What number are you left with?

1	2	3	4	5	6	7
8	9	10	11	12	13	14
15	16	17	18	19	20	21
22	23	24	25	26	27	28
29	30	31	32	33	34	35

Is it an ODD number? .... YES
Can it be divided by 5? .... NO
Is it a PRIME number? .... NO
Are there two figures in the number? .... YES
Can it be divided by 7? .... NO
Do the two figures add up to 6? .... NO

TASK 5 Each coin is placed in one of the boxes.

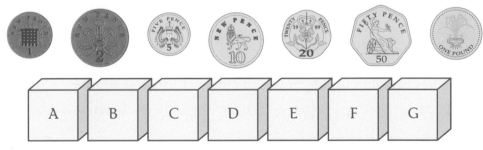

The boxes are shuffled around:

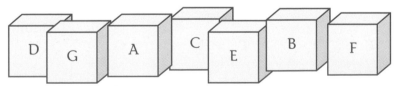

From the clues below, work out which box each coin is in.
1. The box containing the **£1** coin has been moved from the middle to one end.
2. The box containing the **10p** has not been moved at all.
3. One of the boxes that was next to box **E** contains the **2p** coin. It is now next to box **B**.
4. The box with the **50p** inside was on one end. It has moved to the *left*.
5. The box holding the **20p** has been moved two places to the *right*.
6. The box containing the **5p** was moved to the *centre*.

WHICH LONDON BRIDGE?

Use the map of London's bridges and the clues to work out which bridge is which.
If you think that bridge 'A' is Lambeth Bridge, write 'A is Lambeth Bridge'.

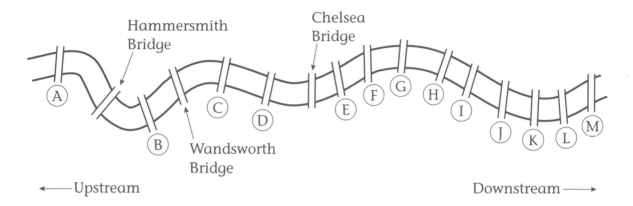

Hammersmith Bridge

Chelsea Bridge

Wandsworth Bridge

←——Upstream   Downstream——→

Here are the bridges that you must find.

Chiswick – Waterloo – Tower – London – Putney
Battersea – Albert – Westminster – Queen Elizabeth II
Southwark – Vauxhall – Lambeth – Blackfriars

Clues:

The bridge <u>upstream</u> from Hammersmith Bridge is **Chiswick Bridge**.

The bridge furthest <u>downstream</u> is the **Queen Elizabeth II Bridge**.

The next bridge <u>upstream</u> from this is **Tower Bridge**.

The bridge <u>upstream</u> from Tower Bridge is **London Bridge**.

The bridge between Hammersmith Bridge and Wandsworth Bridge is **Putney Bridge**.

If you go <u>downstream</u> from Wandsworth Bridge you first pass **Battersea Bridge** and then the **Albert Bridge**.

If you go <u>upstream</u> from London Bridge You find **Southwark Bridge**.

Vauxhall Bridge is found between Chelsea Bridge and **Lambeth Bridge**.

After Lambeth Bridge comes **Westminster Bridge**.

<u>Upstream</u> from Southwark Bridge is **Blackfriars Bridge**.

Between Westminster Bridge and Blackfriars Bridge is **Waterloo Bridge**.

A PUZZLE

The Incredible 'Guess Your Age' Machine.

There are five screens on the machine.
On each screen is a group of numbers from 1 to 30.
Look for the screen or screens that display your age, then count up all the stars above those screens. The number of stars will be equal to your age.

Try this again with a partner. See if you can find their shoe size, their favourite number (between 1 and 30), or their birth date.

② ANGLES AND TURNS

This unit will help you to:
→ **improve your addition and subtraction skills**
→ **understand angles and turning up to 360°**
→ **solve problems involving angles.**

TARGET 180

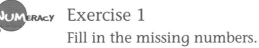 Exercise 1

Fill in the missing numbers.

1. $120 + \boxed{?} = 180$

2. $40 + \boxed{?} = 180$

3. $\boxed{?} + 70 = 180$

4. $\boxed{?} + 110 = 180$

5. $95 + \boxed{?} = 180$

6. $\boxed{?} + 57 = 180$

NUMERACY Exercise 2

Bertha the baby
elephant weighs 180 kg.
What combinations
of weights can you
use to balance Bertha?

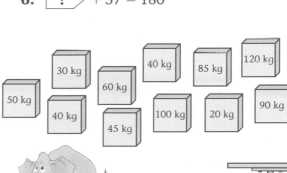

30 kg   40 kg   85 kg   120 kg
50 kg   60 kg   100 kg   90 kg
40 kg   45 kg   20 kg

Example
$120\,kg + 40\,kg + 20\,kg = 180\,kg$

NUMERACY Exercise 3

These number squares all total 180. Copy and complete them.

1.

30	50	80
30	70	
60		180

2.

10	60	
100	10	
110		180

3.

25	45	
75	35	

4.

63	17	
45	55	

5.

40	90	
	30	50
60		

6.

	30	110
40		
120		180

7.

45		
	35	55
65		

8.

	35	
61	50	
95		180

Exercise 4

The toy fire fighter stands on a ladder.
The ladder can turn through 180°, (half a turn).

Use a protractor to measure the angles and
complete the sentences.
The first one is done for you.

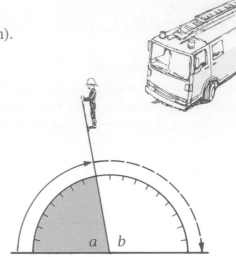

1.

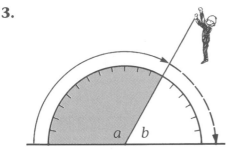

Angle a is <u>50</u> degrees.
Angle b is <u>130</u> degrees.

Angle *a* added to angle *b*
equals <u>180</u> degrees.

2.

Angle a is ___ degrees.
Angle b is ___ degrees.

Angle *a* added to angle *b*
equals ___ degrees.

3.

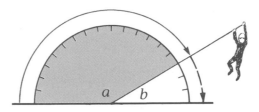

Angle a is ___ degrees.
Angle b is ___ degrees.

Angle *a* added to angle *b*
equals ___ degrees.

4.

Angle a is ___ degrees.
Angle b is ___ degrees.

Angle *a* added to angle *b*
equals ___ degrees.

Remember: the angles on a straight line must add up to 180°.

Exercise 5

Work out the missing angle in each drawing.

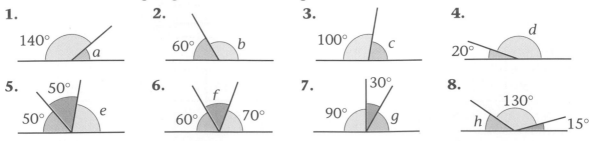

1. 140° *a*

2. 60° *b*

3. 100° *c*

4. *d* 20°

5. 50° 50° *e*

6. 60° *f* 70°

7. 30° 90° *g*

8. 130° *h* 15°

ANGLE FACTS

Example

Kenny is using some angle cards.

He notices that when he puts the 50°, 40° and 90° cards along the edge of his ruler, they make a half turn.

Remember: 180° makes a straight line.

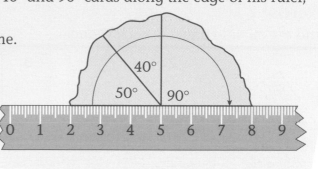

Exercise 6

Use the angle cards to answer these questions.

a Which groups of cards below will form straight lines?
b Add up the angles in the groups that form straight lines.

1. Group A: 40°, 90°, 50°
2. Group B: 130°, 40°
3. Group C: 60°, 120°
4. Group D: 120°, 130°, 50°
5. Group E: 120°, 60°

6. Group F: 50°, 130°
7. Group G: 60°, 30°, 90°
8. Group H: 50°, 60°, 30°, 40°
9. Group I: 20°, 120°, 50°

10. Can you think of your own grouping of these angle cards that will form a straight line?

You can trace and cut out these angle cards if it will help.

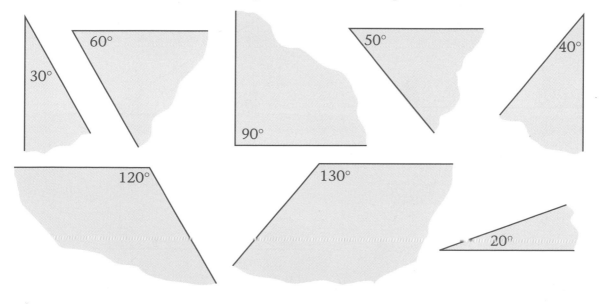

Remember:

The angles of a triangle *always* add up to 180°.

$a + b + c = 180°$

Remember:

The box in the corner shows that the angle is a

right angle = 90°

Exercise 7

Find the missing angle in each triangle.

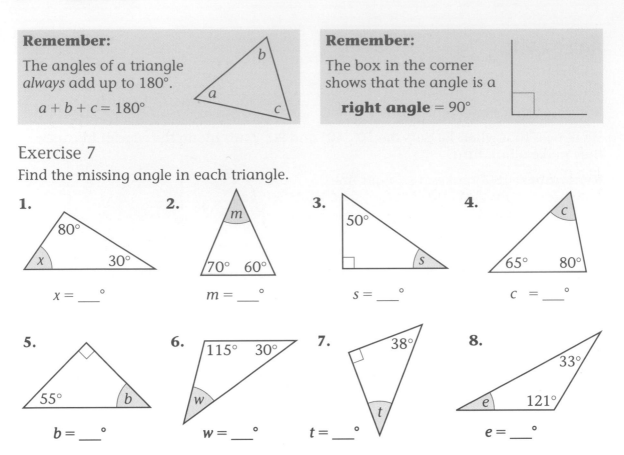

1.
80°
x
30°

$x = \underline{\quad}°$

2.
m
70°   60°

$m = \underline{\quad}°$

3.
50°
s

$s = \underline{\quad}°$

4.
c
65°   80°

$c = \underline{\quad}°$

5.
55°   b

$b = \underline{\quad}°$

6.
115°   30°
w

$w = \underline{\quad}°$

7.
38°
t

$t = \underline{\quad}°$

8.
33°
e   121°

$e = \underline{\quad}°$

Exercise 8

Using what you know about the number of degrees in a triangle, and that there are 180° in a half turn, work out the angles that are missing from these triangular shapes. The first is done for you.

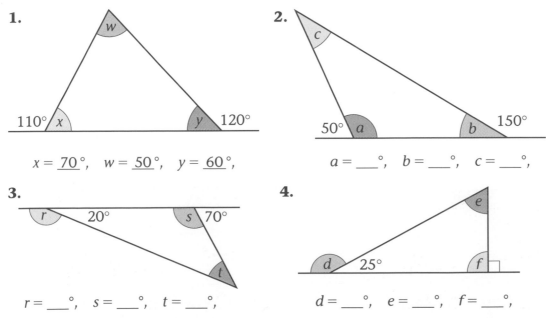

1.
w
110° x   y   120°

$x = \underline{70}°, \quad w = \underline{50}°, \quad y = \underline{60}°,$

2.
c
50° a   b   150°

$a = \underline{\quad}°, \quad b = \underline{\quad}°, \quad c = \underline{\quad}°,$

3.
r   20°   s 70°
t

$r = \underline{\quad}°, \quad s = \underline{\quad}°, \quad t = \underline{\quad}°,$

4.
e
d   25°   f

$d = \underline{\quad}°, \quad e = \underline{\quad}°, \quad f = \underline{\quad}°,$

Remember:

When two lines cross, they create 4 angles. The **opposite** angles are **equal** to each other.

30°   30°

Remember:

When two lines cross, **adjacent** angles **add up to 180°**.

150°   30° = 180°

Exercise 9

Using the information above, give the missing angles.

1.

a   20°

a = ___°

2.

80° m

m = ___°

3.

15°   y

y = ___°

4.

t   120°

t = ___°

5.

s 161°

s = ___°

6.

w   r

50°

r = ___°,   w = ___°,

Exercise 10

Using what you know about **opposite** angles, and the angles in a triangle, work out the missing angles in these shapes.

1.

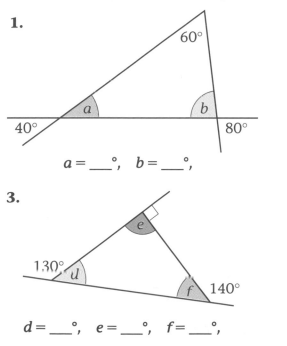

60°

a   b

40°   80°

a = ___°,   b = ___°,

2.

40°

r

t   s

120°   20°

r = ___°,   s = ___°,   t = ___°,

3.

e

130° u

f   140°

d = ___°,   e = ___°,   f = ___°,

4.

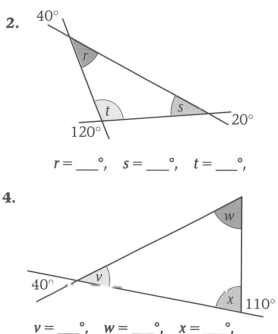

w

40°   v

x 110°

v = ___°,   w = ___°,   x = ___°,

TARGET 360

NUMERACY Exercise 11

All the numbers in these chains must total 360.
Find the missing numbers in each chain.

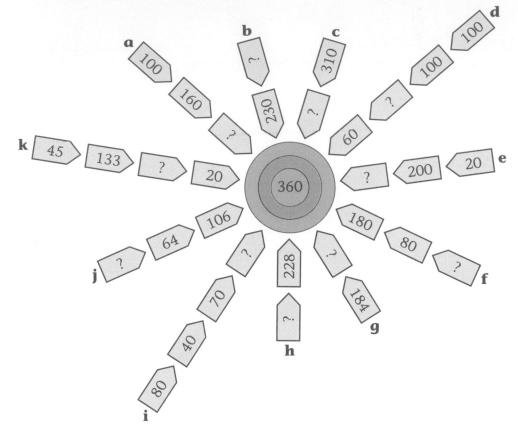

NUMERACY Exercise 12

These number squares all total 360. Copy and complete them.

1.

50	150	200
100	60	
		360

2.

100	100	
80	80	
180		360

3.

130	50	
80	100	
		360

4.

35	135	
95	95	

5.

41	39	
279	1	

6.

130		215
	125	
150	210	

7.

	140	
30		160
	270	360

8.

35		170
	95	
	230	360

ANGLES AND TURNING

Jenny takes her little brother Tommy to the park. She puts him on the roundabout and slowly turns it.

Below you can see Tommy turning on the roundabout.

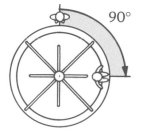 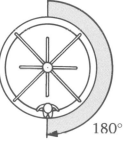 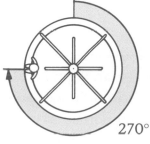 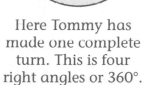

Here Tommy has turned through one right angle or 90°.

Here Tommy has turned through two right angles or 180°.

Here Tommy has turned through three right angles or 270°.

Here Tommy has made one complete turn. This is four right angles or 360°.

Remember: There are 360° or four right angles in one turn.

Exercise 13

How many more degrees of turn are needed to complete one turn or 360°.

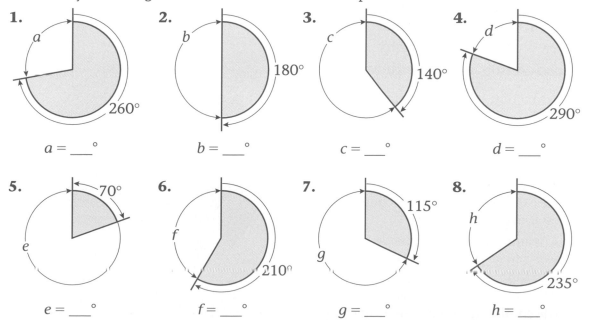

1. 260° $a =$ ___°
2. 180° $b =$ ___°
3. 140° $c =$ ___°
4. 290° $d =$ ___°

5. 70° $e =$ ___°
6. 210° $f =$ ___°
7. 115° $g =$ ___°
8. 235° $h =$ ___°

THE COMPASS ROSE

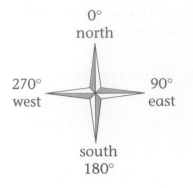

This is a compass rose. It shows the positions north, east, south and west.

The angle between each of the four compass points is 90° or one right angle.

We always count angles on a compass in a clockwise direction starting from north (0°).
So east is 90° from north, south is 180° from north and so on.

Exercise 14

Copy and complete the sentences below.

1. There are ___° between north and east.
2. There are ___° between north and south.
3. There are ___° between north and west.
4. One full turn is ___° or ___ right angles.
5. From east to south is ___° (remember to turn clockwise).
6. From east to north is ___°.
7. If you turn from south to north, you turn through ___°.
8. There are ___° from west to south.
9. One half of a full turn is ___° or ___ right angles.

Exercise 15

Mary is standing in the middle of this roundabout.
What will she see if she looks:

1. east
2. north
3. south-west
4. north-west?

What direction is Mary facing
if she can see:

5. Cliff Road
6. Ice Lane
7. The Station
8. Castle Street?

9. A man standing outside the Station sees Mary. In which direction is he looking?

10. A woman standing outside the Museum sees Mary. In which direction is she looking?

11. Wallace Way is a one-way street. In which direction does the traffic travel?

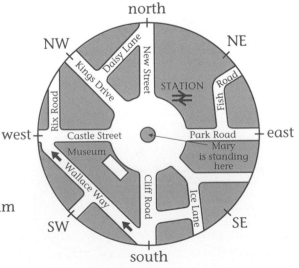

Exercise 16

Use this compass rose to complete these sentences.

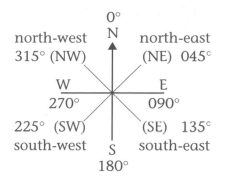

1. There are ___° between north and north-east.
2. There are ___° between north and south-east.
3. From north to north-west is ___°.
4. From north-east to south-east is ___°.
5. There are ___° between south-east and north-west.
6. If you turn from west to north-east you have turned through ___°.
7. Complete the sentences below using either the word 'more' or the word 'less'.

   a A turn from north to north-east is ___ than one right angle.

   b The angle between south-west and east is ___ than two right angles.

   c From north to north-west is ___ than four right angles.

   d A full turn is ___ than three right angles.

Exercise 17

Here is the radar screen on HMS Tiger.
It shows other ships, objects and land.
HMS Tiger is heading on a bearing of 090°.
Use a ruler to help you work
out the bearings of the
following points from HMS Tiger.

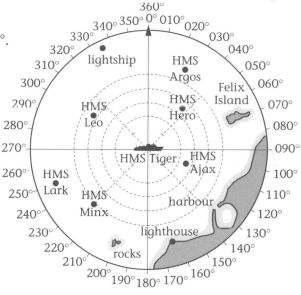

Object	Bearing
HMS Argos	___°
Felix Island	___°
rocks	___°
HMS Lark	___°
HMS Hero	___°
lightship	___°
_____	225°
_____	300°
_____	110°
_____	165°

1. The harbour is on a bearing of ___°.
2. How many ships are sailing north of HMS Tiger?
3. What will happen if HMS Tiger continues on a course of 090°?
4. Which ship is roughly north-west of HMS Tiger?

③ How Much Do You Know?

This unit will test how much you know using 100 questions.

A. Decimals

What decimal part of each shape is coloured?

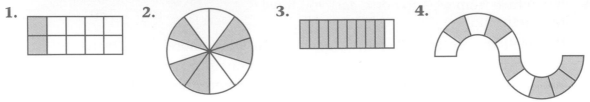

1.   **2.**   **3.**   **4.**

Write down the decimals that are shown on this number line.

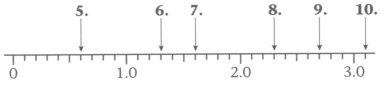

Re-write these decimals in order. Start with the smallest.

11. 0.9, 0.7, 1.5   **12.** 1.7, 0.8, 2.5, 0.1   **13.** 0.2, 0.0, 2.0, 3.1, 1.7

B. Angles and shape

Which angles are larger than a right angle?
Which angles are smaller than a right angle?
Copy the table below and write the number of each angle in the correct column.

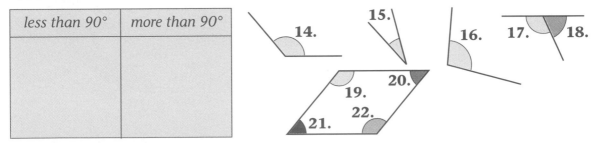

less than 90°	more than 90°

Copy and complete the table below giving the order of rotation for each shape.
(The order of rotation is the number of times a shape looks the same during one rotation.)

Shape	Order of rotation
23.	
24.	
25.	

C. TRIANGLES

What is the size of each angle marked with a letter?

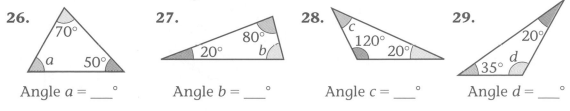

26. Angle a = ___°

27. Angle b = ___°

28. Angle c = ___°

29. Angle d = ___°

Without measuring the angles or sides, say whether these triangles are:
scalene, **isosceles**, **equilateral** or **right angle**.

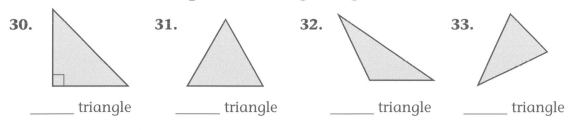

30. _____ triangle

31. _____ triangle

32. _____ triangle

33. _____ triangle

D. FRACTIONS

Say what fraction of the whole has been coloured in each drawing.

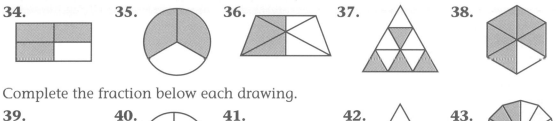

34. **35.** **36.** **37.** **38.**

Complete the fraction below each drawing.

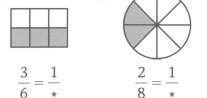

39. $\frac{3}{6} = \frac{1}{*}$

40. $\frac{2}{8} = \frac{1}{*}$

41. $\frac{*}{15} = \frac{1}{3}$

42. $\frac{3}{9} = \frac{1}{*}$

43. $\frac{9}{*} = \frac{*}{4}$

E. COORDINATES

44. What would you hit at coordinate (3, 1)?

45. What vessel would you hit at coordinate (6, 1)?

46. Give a coordinate to hit the patrol boat.

47. Give three coordinates that hit the destroyer.

48. Give five coordinates that hit the aircraft carrier.

49. Give two coordinates to hit the submarine.

50. Which vessel is closest to coordinate (0, 4)?

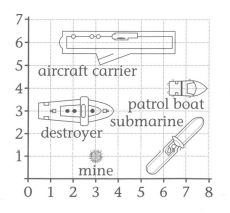

F. Area

Find the area of each shape below.

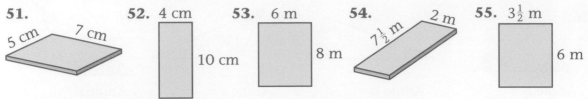

51. 5 cm 7 cm

52. 4 cm 10 cm

53. 6 m 8 m

54. $7\frac{1}{2}$ m 2 m

55. $3\frac{1}{2}$ m 6 m

Find the length of the sides marked with a question mark.

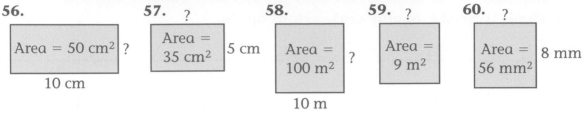

56. Area = 50 cm² ? 10 cm

57. ? Area = 35 cm² 5 cm

58. Area = 100 m² ? 10 m

59. ? Area = 9 m²

60. ? Area = 56 mm² 8 mm

Give the area of each triangle.

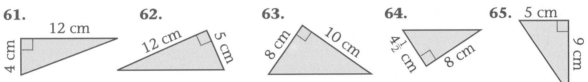

61. 12 cm 4 cm

62. 12 cm 5 cm

63. 8 cm 10 cm

64. $4\frac{1}{2}$ cm 8 cm

65. 5 cm 9 cm

G. Distance

Copy and complete the village sign posts, and answer the questions.

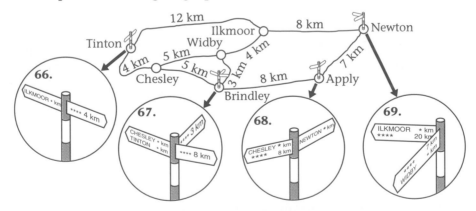

70. How far is it from Chesley to Apply, going by Brindley?

71. How far is it from Newton to Brindley, going by Apply?

72. How far is it from Tinton to Apply, going by the shortest route?

73. How far is it from Chesley to Newton, going by the shortest route?

74. How many different ways are there to get from Newton to Chesley?

75. Janice walks at 5 km per hour. How many hours does it take her to walk from Tinton to Newton by the shortest route?

H. NUMBER PATTERNS

Copy these factor trees and fill in the missing numbers.

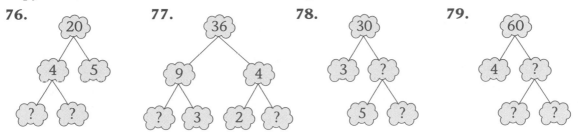

76.   **77.**   **78.**   **79.**

Find all the factor pairs of the numbers below.

Example: 12 = 12 × 1 = 3 × 4 = 6 × 2

80. 30   **81.** 21   **82.** 45   **83.** 17   **84.** 40

85. Which number above has only one factor pair? This number is a prime number.

86. Which of the numbers below are prime numbers?

4, 6, 9, 13, 15, 19, 20, 21, 23, 27, 31

I. TIME

87. Toby starts running at time A.
He finishes running at time B.
How long was he running for?

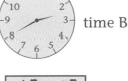

88. An airliner leaves Frankfurt at time X.
It arrives at Gatwick at time Y.
How long was the journey?

time X   time Y

From the time shown on this clock:

89. add 20 minutes

90. add half an hour

91. subtract 3 hours

92. subtract 1 hour and 5 minutes

From the time shown on this clock:

93. add 30 minutes

94. add 1 hour and 25 minutes

95. subtract 2 hours

96. subtract 1 hour and 15 minutes

Convert these 12-hour clock times to 24-hour clock times.

97. 11.20 a.m.   **98.** 8.30 p.m.   **99.** 11.20 p.m.   **100.** 1.15 a.m.

4 ESTIMATION AND ROUNDING OFF

Key words

estimate
round off
near
nearer
nearest

This unit will help you to:
→ **make estimates by sight**
→ **make sensible calculations in your head**
→ **round off numbers.**

Guess the weight of the cake

HOW MANY PEAS

ESTIMATING

An estimate is an approximate or rough calculation –
it is not a wild guess.
At a fete you could be asked to guess the weight of a
cake or the number of peas in a jar.

You cannot count the peas or weigh the cake, so all you can do is make an estimate.

Exercise 1

Give an estimated answer to these problems.

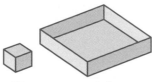

How many cubes
do you think would
fit in the tray?

How many people
do you think are
on the big dipper?

How many children
do you think are
in the playground?

Estimating gives a rough idea of what an answer should be.

Exercise 2

Give an estimated answer to each of these questions.
1. How tall are you?
2. What is your weight?
3. How long does it take you to travel to school?
4. How far is your home from the school?
5. How many students are there in your school?
6. How many teachers are there in your school?
7. How many seats are there on a double-decker bus?
8. How many hours per week do you spend asleep?

You can make an estimate of the number shown on the dial.
The dial on the right shows about 2.4

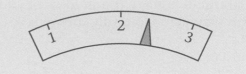

Exercise 3

Estimate the number shown on each dial below.

1.

2.

3.

4.

5.

6.

7.

8.

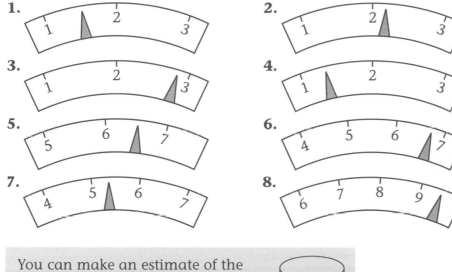

You can make an estimate of the amount in a container
This container is about $\frac{1}{2}$ full.

Exercise 4

Estimate the amount in each of the containers below.
Choose your answer from the fractions shown in the brackets.

1.

This fish tank is about ___ full. ($\frac{1}{2}$, $\frac{1}{10}$, $\frac{1}{3}$)

2.

This jug is about ___ full. ($\frac{1}{4}$, $\frac{2}{3}$, $\frac{1}{3}$)

3.

This mug is about ___ full. ($\frac{3}{4}$, $\frac{1}{5}$, $\frac{1}{2}$)

4.

This beaker is about ___ full. ($\frac{1}{4}$, $\frac{1}{3}$, $\frac{1}{10}$)

5.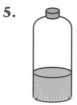

This bottle is about ___ full. ($\frac{2}{5}$, $\frac{2}{3}$, $\frac{3}{4}$)

6.

This jar is about ___ full. ($\frac{4}{5}$, $\frac{1}{4}$, $\frac{1}{2}$)

It is useful to have a 'rough idea' of your answer before you start a calculation.
In this way you avoid silly answers.

Exercise 5

For each of these bills, decide which estimated total is most accurate.

1. **a** 'I think the total is about £3.00'
   b 'I think the total is about £6.00'
   c 'I think the total is about £4.00'

2. **a** 'I think the total is about £12.00'
   b 'I think the total is about £9.00'
   c 'I think the total is about £10.00'

3. **a** 'I think the total is about £6.00'
   b 'I think the total is about £7.50'
   c 'I think the total is about £8.50'

4. **a** 'I think the total is about £33.00'
   b 'I think the total is about £28.00'
   c 'I think the total is about £39.00'

5. **a** 'I think the total is about £412.50'
   b 'I think the total is about £32.00'
   c 'I think the total is about £36.50'

Exercise 6

Estimate which answer is accurate.

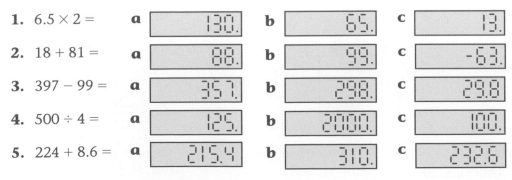

1. $6.5 \times 2 =$ **a** `130.`   **b** `65.`   **c** `13.`
2. $18 + 81 =$ **a** `88.`   **b** `99.`   **c** `-63.`
3. $397 - 99 =$ **a** `357.`   **b** `298.`   **c** `29.8`
4. $500 \div 4 =$ **a** `125.`   **b** `2000.`   **c** `100.`
5. $224 + 8.6 =$ **a** `215.4`   **b** `310.`   **c** `232.6`

Exercise 7

In this chess set the bishop is 9 cm tall.
Use this information to estimate the height of the other chess pieces.

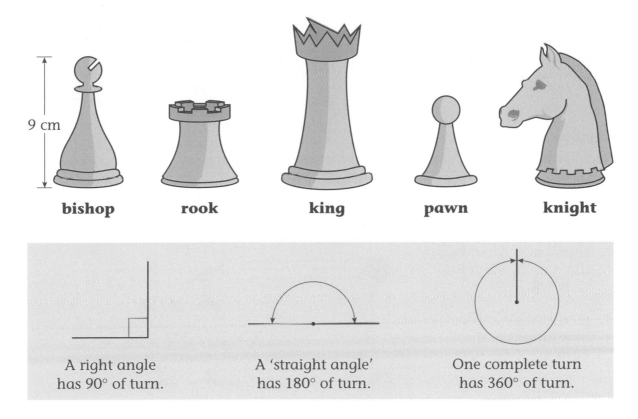

| **bishop** | **rook** | **king** | **pawn** | **knight** |

A right angle
has 90° of turn.

A 'straight angle'
has 180° of turn.

One complete turn
has 360° of turn.

Exercise 8

Using the information above decide which estimate is the most accurate.

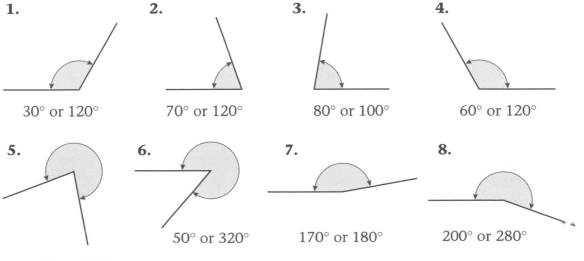

1.
30° or 120°

2.
70° or 120°

3.
80° or 100°

4.
60° or 120°

5.
170° or 280°

6.
50° or 320°

7.
170° or 180°

8.
200° or 280°

ROUNDING

There are times when it is useful to give an answer that has been rounded off.

Example

Liza asked two people for the time.
One answer was very accurate,
the other answer was rounded off

Exercise 9

Decide which answer, A or B, has been rounded off.

1. Mr Brown asks the
   Green twins their age.

2. Hamil asks two men at
   the station, when the
   train will arrive.

3. Jenny asks two people
   how far it is to the
   bank.

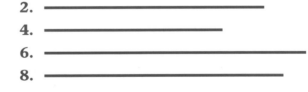

Exercise 10

Measure these lines and round off your answers to the nearest centimetre.

1. ────────────   2. ──────────────

3. ────   4. ─────────────

5. ──────   6. ───────────────

7. ──────   8. ──────────────

Exercise 11

Round off these times to the nearest hour, half hour or quarter hour.
The first one is done for you.

It is about a
quarter to 3.

ROUNDING TO THE NEAREST TEN, HUNDRED OR THOUSAND

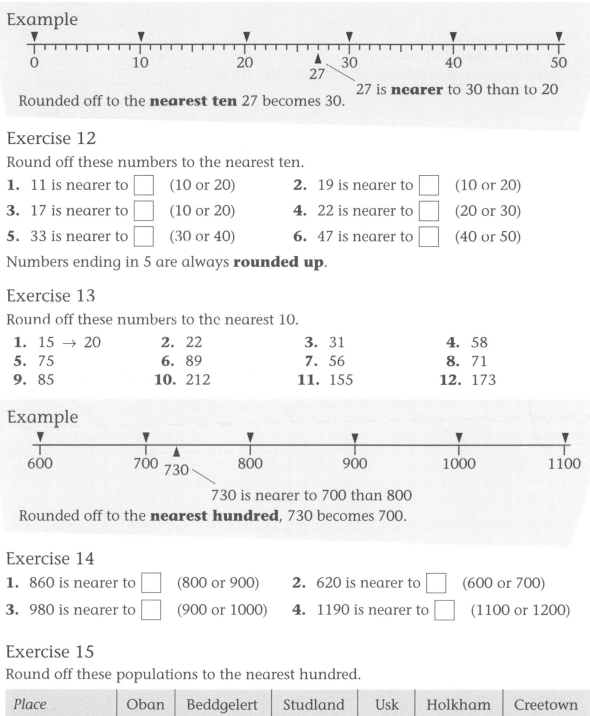

Example

Rounded off to the **nearest ten** 27 becomes 30.

27 is **nearer** to 30 than to 20

Exercise 12

Round off these numbers to the nearest ten.

1. 11 is nearer to ☐ (10 or 20)   **2.** 19 is nearer to ☐ (10 or 20)

3. 17 is nearer to ☐ (10 or 20)   **4.** 22 is nearer to ☐ (20 or 30)

5. 33 is nearer to ☐ (30 or 40)   **6.** 47 is nearer to ☐ (40 or 50)

Numbers ending in 5 are always **rounded up**.

Exercise 13

Round off these numbers to the nearest 10.

1. 15 → 20	**2.** 22	**3.** 31	**4.** 58
5. 75	**6.** 89	**7.** 56	**8.** 71
9. 85	**10.** 212	**11.** 155	**12.** 173

Example

730 is nearer to 700 than 800

Rounded off to the **nearest hundred**, 730 becomes 700.

Exercise 14

1. 860 is nearer to ☐ (800 or 900)   **2.** 620 is nearer to ☐ (600 or 700)

3. 980 is nearer to ☐ (900 or 1000)   **4.** 1190 is nearer to ☐ (1100 or 1200)

Exercise 15

Round off these populations to the nearest hundred.

Place	Oban	Beddgelert	Studland	Usk	Holkham	Creetown
Population	8134	671	620	1890	272	785
Rounded off	8100					

⑤ PARALLEL LINES

Key words

parallel

concentric

This unit will help you to:
➔ **recognise parallel lines**
➔ **make angle calculations about parallel lines.**

In each pair of lines, line A is **parallel** to line B.

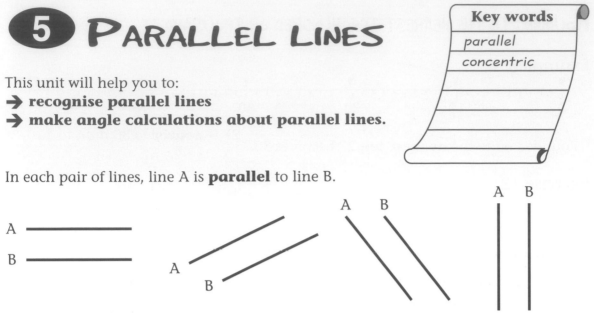

Lines that are parallel to each other are the same distance apart at each end, and they will never get closer together.

These pairs of lines are not parallel to each other.

These circles are not parallel.
Parallel lines are straight.
The circles are concentric.
They have the same centre.

Exercise 1

Say which pairs of lines are parallel. You can use a ruler to measure or you can judge 'by eye'.

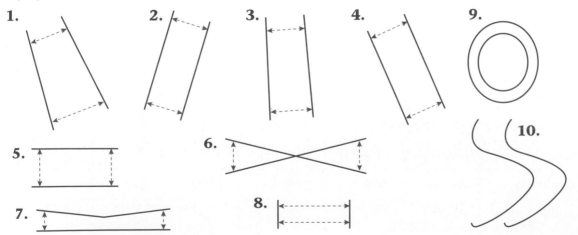

TASK 1 Find which line, **a**, **b**, **c** or **d** is parallel to the line drawn in red, in each group.

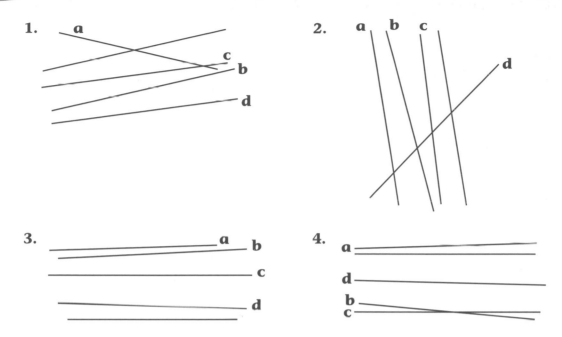

5. Draw three lines that are parallel to each other.
Each line should be about 8 cm long. Leave about 3 cm between each line.
The drawing should look like this:
This drawing is not full size.

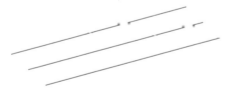

6. One pair of heavy lines below are not parallel to each other. Which pair is it?

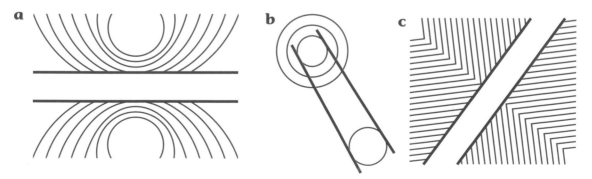

7. Explain how you got your answer. If you judged 'by eye', how could you be more accurate?

TASK 2 The questions below will help you to discover facts about parallel lines and angles. Use a protractor to measure the angles.

1. Can you tell by looking that the lines A and B are parallel?

   a Angle $a = $ ___°

   b Angle $b = $ ___°

   c What do you notice about the two angles?

2. In the drawing below, check whether the angles made by the two parallel lines are equal.

3. Copy and complete this statement:
   When a straight line crosses two parallel lines, the angles that they make are _____.

4. It is difficult to judge whether or not these lines are parallel by just looking. Use a protractor to measure the angles.
   Say which lines are parallel to each other.

ANGLES AND PARALLEL LINES

Exercise 2

Use what you know about angles and parallel lines to say which pairs of red lines would be parallel to each other.
(Do not try to judge by eyesight, the drawings have been drawn incorrectly)

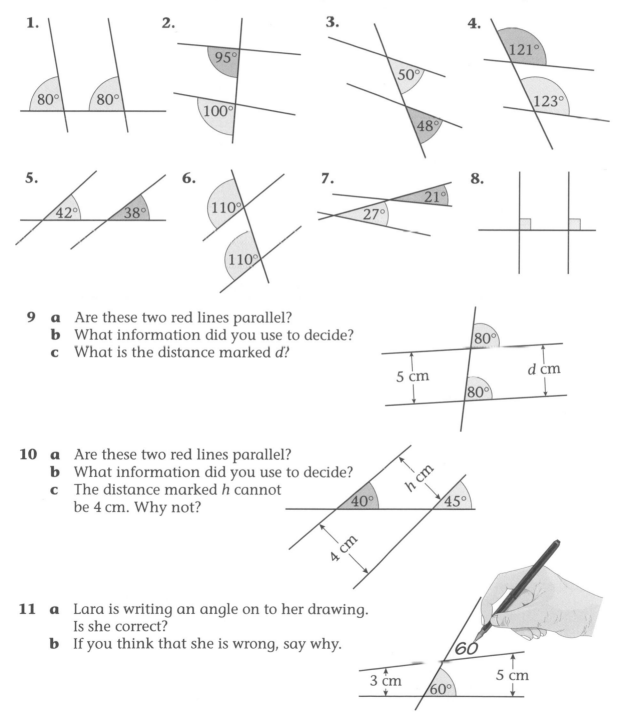

1.

80°   80°

2.

95°
100°

3.

50°
48°

4.

121°
123°

5.

42°   38°

6.

110°
110°

7.

21°
27°

8.

9 **a** Are these two red lines parallel?
   b What information did you use to decide?
   c What is the distance marked *d*?

80°
5 cm   *d* cm
80°

10 **a** Are these two red lines parallel?
   b What information did you use to decide?
   c The distance marked *h* cannot
      be 4 cm. Why not?

h cm
40°   45°
4 cm

11 **a** Lara is writing an angle on to her drawing.
      Is she correct?
   b If you think that she is wrong, say why.

60
3 cm   5 cm
60°

6 THE FOUR RULES OF NUMBER

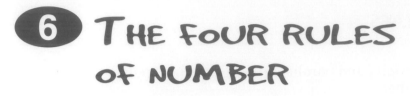

Key words

ratio

pattern

This unit will help you to:
→ **practice the Four Rules of number**
→ **use different strategies in calculations**
→ **solve problems involving the Four Rules.**

ADDITION AND SUBTRACTION

Addition workcard 1

1. $206 + 153 =$ 2. $317 + 302 =$
3. $660 + 128 =$ 4. $235 + 350 =$
5. $129 + 212 =$ 6. $228 + 235 =$
7. $547 + 127 =$ 8. $416 + 448 =$

Addition workcard 2

1. $180 + 453 =$ 2. $292 + 161 =$
3. $376 + 482 =$ 4. $188 + 350 =$
5. $450 + 196 =$ 6. $687 + 72 =$
7. $66 + 273 =$ 8. $658 + 80 =$

Addition workcard 3

1. $23 + 34 + 22 =$ 2. $45 + 32 + 12 =$
3. $10 + 48 + 21 =$ 4. $23 + 51 + 21 =$
5. $16 + 43 + 22 =$ 6. $38 + 44 + 14 =$
7. $17 + 45 + 23 =$ 8. $17 + 20 + 39 =$

Addition workcard 4

1. $48 + 19 + 15 =$ 2. $27 + 17 + 48 =$
3. $18 + 37 + 19 =$ 4. $49 + 17 + 27 =$
5. $59 + 5 + 37 =$ 6. $28 + 27 + 8 =$
7. $38 + 38 + 14 =$ 8. $47 + 64 + 29 =$

Subtraction workcard 1

1. $88 - 15 =$ 2. $74 - 53 =$
3. $68 - 25 =$ 4. $47 - 23 =$
5. $78 - 38 =$ 6. $57 - 55 =$
7. $86 - 56 =$ 8. $64 - 63 =$

Subtraction workcard 2

1. $80 - 15 =$ 2. $70 - 36 =$
3. $60 - 23 =$ 4. $72 - 16 =$
5. $51 - 14 =$ 6. $34 - 17 =$
7. $76 - 39 =$ 8. $85 - 48 =$

Subtraction workcard 3

1. $272 - 126 =$ 2. $580 - 128 =$
3. $853 - 227 =$ 4. $681 - 177 =$
5. $634 - 286 =$ 6. $513 - 263 =$
7. $705 - 340 =$ 8. $636 - 250 =$

Subtraction workcard 4

1. $451 - 246 =$ 2. $360 - 255 =$
3. $512 - 305 =$ 4. $873 - 267 =$
5. $742 - 156 =$ 6. $422 - 236 =$
7. $632 - 274 =$ 8. $420 - 156 =$

Exercise 1

Use your addition and subtraction skills to answer these problems.

  1. What is 20 + 30 + 40 + 50?
  2. Take 55 from 98.
  3. Add 67 to 138.
  4. What is 100, subtract 37?
  5. What is 108, plus 255?
  6. What is 161, take away 88?
  7. Add 155, 246 and 36.
  8. Take 78 from 113.
  9. Which is greater: 55 + 44 or 142 − 44?
 10. Find the total of 15 + 16 + 17 and take this total from 73.
 11.

94 cm

57 cm is cut from this length of tape. What length of tape will be left?

 12.

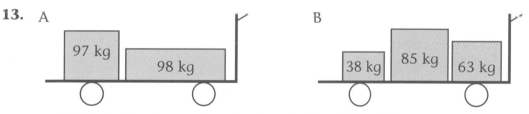

£13   £38   £21   £18

   a How much money is there, in total, in these four 'piggy' banks?
   b If £25 is taken from this total, how much will be left?

 13. A   B

97 kg   98 kg   38 kg   85 kg   63 kg

   a Which trolley is carrying the heavier load, A or B?
   b What is the difference in weight between the two trolleys?

 14.

115 km

49 km — 34 km

Carlisle   Appleby   Garsdale   Settle

   a How far is it from Carlisle to Garsdale?
   b How far is it from Garsdale to Settle?

 15. a What is the difference in weight between
             the two boxes?
   b What is the total weight of the two boxes?

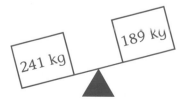

241 kg   189 kg

MULTIPLICATION METHODS

When you multiply a number by 10 you move its digits one **place** to the left.

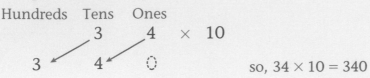

Example

Hundreds	Tens	Ones
	3	4 × 10
3	4	0

so, 34 × 10 = 340

Exercise 2

Use your calculator to answer these problems involving multiplying by 10.
Do them as quickly as you can.

1. 4 × 10 =   **2.** 14 × 10 =   **3.** 23 × 10 =   **4.** 37 × 10 =

5. 53 × 10 =   **6.** 62 × 10 =   **7.** 70 × 10 =   **8.** 94 × 10 =

9. 243 × 10 =   **10.** 418 × 10 =   **11.** 608 × 10 =   **12.** 370 × 10 =

Exercise 3

Work out these problems involving multiplying by 10.
Do *not* use a calculator.

1. 7 × 10 =   **2.** 9 × 10 =   **3.** 13 × 10 =   **4.** 26 × 10 =

5. 61 × 10 =   **6.** 85 × 10 =   **7.** 88 × 10 =   **8.** 90 × 10 =

9. 262 × 10 =   **10.** 502 × 10 =   **11.** 640 × 10 =   **12.** 300 × 10 =

13. a   What do you notice about all of your answers so far?
    b   What is your short cut for multiplying whole numbers by ten?

Exercise 4

These problems all involve multiplying by 10.
Use your short cut to write down the answers.

1.

Here are 7 boxes.
There are 10 sweets in each box.
How many sweets are there in total?

2.

Here are 10 minibuses.
Each bus is carrying 17 people.
How many people are there in all?

3. A gas pipe is 12 metres long. If 10 pipes are laid end to end, how many metres would they stretch?

4. A crate holds 10 bottles. How many bottles are there in 27 crates?

5. A sack of potatoes weighs 25 kilograms.
How much would 10 sacks weigh?

USING MULTIPLICATION BY 10

By now you should have a quick way to multiply any whole number by 10.

You can use the short cut to multiply by other numbers.

To multiply 15 by 9, I multiply by 10, then take off one of the 15's.

step 1:
15 × 10 = 150

step 2:
take away   15
                135

so:
15 × 9 = 135 ✓

Exercise 5

Try the method above to do these multiplications.

1. 14 × 9 =
step 1: × by 10
step 2: take away 14

2. 13 × 9 =
step 1: × by 10
step 2: take away 13

3. 18 × 9 =
step 1: × by 10
step 2: take away 18

4. 19 × 9 =
step 1: × by 10
step 2: take away 19

5. 17 × 9 =
step 1: × by 10
step 2: take away 17

6. 25 × 9 =
step 1: × by 10
step 2: take away 25

7. 22 × 9 =
step 1: × by 10
step 2: take away 22

8. 20 × 9 =
step 1: × by 10
step 2: take away 20

9. 16 × 9 =
step 1: × by 10
step 2: take away 16

You can use the same method to multiply by 8.
For 15 × 8 =   step 1: 15 × 10   step 2: take away two 15s

10. Finish the multiplication above.

11. 25 × 8 =
step 1: × by 10
step 2: take away
two 25s

12. 14 × 8 =
step 1: × by 10
step 2: take away
two 14s

13. 30 × 8 =
step 1: × by 10
step 2: take away
two 30s

MULTIPLYING BY TENS AND UNITS

This is another way to multiply by bigger numbers. You split the tens and units, and multiply them separately, then add the two answers together.

To multiply 16 × 9, split the 16 into 10 and 6. Multiply the 10 by 9. Put the answer into the box.

Do the same for 6 × 9.

Now add the two answers together.

16 × 9

10	6

10 × 9 = 90	6 × 9 = 54	9

$$10 \times 9 = 90$$
$$+\ 6 \times 9 = 54$$
$$16 \times 9 = 144$$

Exercise 6

The multiplications below show how the tens and units are split.
Finish the multiplications by filling in the spaces.

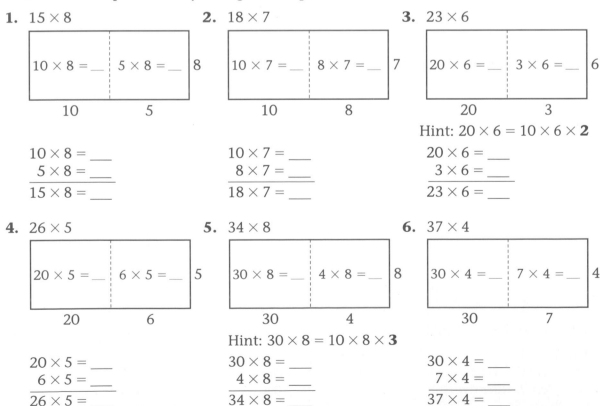

1. 15 × 8

10 × 8 = __	5 × 8 = __	8

10   5

$$10 \times 8 = \underline{}$$
$$5 \times 8 = \underline{}$$
$$15 \times 8 = \underline{}$$

2. 18 × 7

10 × 7 = __	8 × 7 = __	7

10   8

$$10 \times 7 = \underline{}$$
$$8 \times 7 = \underline{}$$
$$18 \times 7 = \underline{}$$

3. 23 × 6

20 × 6 = __	3 × 6 = __	6

20   3

Hint: 20 × 6 = 10 × 6 × **2**

$$20 \times 6 = \underline{}$$
$$3 \times 6 = \underline{}$$
$$23 \times 6 = \underline{}$$

4. 26 × 5

20 × 5 = __	6 × 5 = __	5

20   6

$$20 \times 5 = \underline{}$$
$$6 \times 5 = \underline{}$$
$$26 \times 5 = \underline{}$$

5. 34 × 8

30 × 8 = __	4 × 8 = __	8

30   4

Hint: 30 × 8 = 10 × 8 × **3**

$$30 \times 8 = \underline{}$$
$$4 \times 8 = \underline{}$$
$$34 \times 8 = \underline{}$$

6. 37 × 4

30 × 4 = __	7 × 4 = __	4

30   7

$$30 \times 4 = \underline{}$$
$$7 \times 4 = \underline{}$$
$$37 \times 4 = \underline{}$$

7. 18×6

$10 \times 6 =$ ___	$8 \times 6 =$ ___

     10   8

$10 \times 6 =$ ___
$8 \times 6 =$ ___
$18 \times 6 =$ ___

8. 19×8

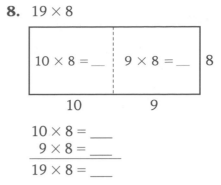

$10 \times 8 =$ ___	$9 \times 8 =$ ___

     10   9

$10 \times 8 =$ ___
$9 \times 8 =$ ___
$19 \times 8 =$ ___

9. 25×7

$20 \times 7 =$ ___	$5 \times 7 =$ ___

     20   5

$20 \times 7 =$ ___
$5 \times 7 =$ ___
$25 \times 7 =$ ___

10. 23×4

$20 \times 4 =$ ___	$3 \times 4 =$ ___

     20   3

$20 \times 4 =$ ___
$3 \times 4 =$ ___
$23 \times 4 =$ ___

11. 38×6

$30 \times 6 =$ ___	$8 \times 6 =$ ___

     30   8

$30 \times 6 =$ ___
$8 \times 6 =$ ___
$38 \times 6 =$ ___

12. 67×3

$60 \times 3 =$ ___	$7 \times 3 =$ ___

     60   7

$60 \times 3 =$ ___
$7 \times 3 =$ ___
$67 \times 3 =$ ___

Use a method that works for you to complete these multiplication problems.

Multiplication workcard 1

1. $13 \times 7 =$	**2.** $17 \times 5 =$
3. $12 \times 9 =$	**4.** $15 \times 9 =$
5. $18 \times 6 =$	**6.** $19 \times 6 =$
7. $25 \times 5 =$	**8.** $28 \times 7 =$
9. $23 \times 6 =$	**10.** $26 \times 8 =$

Multiplication workcard 2

1. $34 \times 6 =$	**2.** $45 \times 5 =$
3. $32 \times 9 =$	**4.** $43 \times 8 =$
5. $38 \times 7 =$	**6.** $47 \times 6 =$
7. $55 \times 6 =$	**8.** $68 \times 4 =$
9. $72 \times 7 =$	**10.** $92 \times 5 =$

PATTERNS IN RATIO

Here are 3 green beads and
9 orange beads.

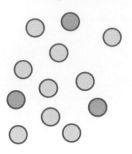

They can be arranged
in a pattern like this:

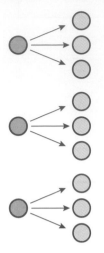

There are 3 orange beads for every green bead, or, one green bead goes with every three orange beads.

Exercise 7

a Redraw each of the groups of beads below, to make a pattern.

b For each pattern, copy and finish these two sentences:
'There are * orange beads for every green bead.'
'One green bead goes with every * orange beads.'

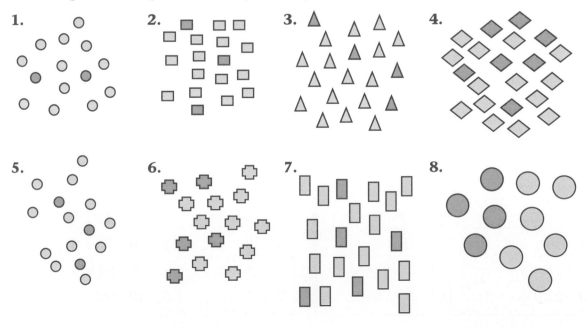

This pattern shows that there are
3 orange beads to every one green bead.

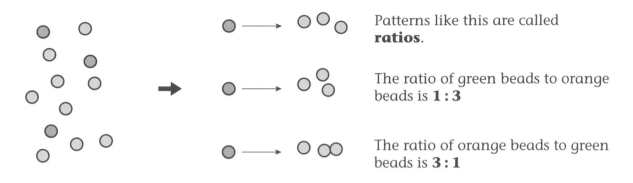

Patterns like this are called
ratios.

The ratio of green beads to orange
beads is **1 : 3**

The ratio of orange beads to green
beads is **3 : 1**

Exercise 8

1. Which patterns below have a ratio of green beads to orange beads of 1 : 3?

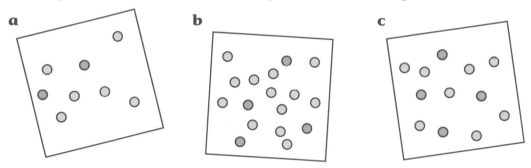

a   b   c

2. Which patterns below have a ratio of green beads to orange beads of 2 : 3?

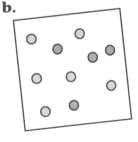

a.   **b.**

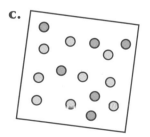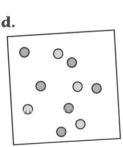

c.   **d.**

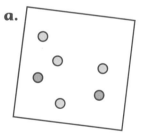

MULTIPLICATION AND RATIO

The orange beads are missing from this ratio pattern.
You can find how many orange beads are needed for a ratio of green to orange 1 : 4.

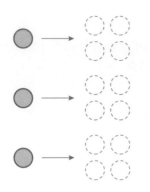

You need 4 orange beads for every green bead.

So you need $3 \times 4 = 12$ orange beads to finish the pattern.

Exercise 9

In each question below, work out how many orange beads are needed to complete the ratio. Use a drawing or counters if it will help you.

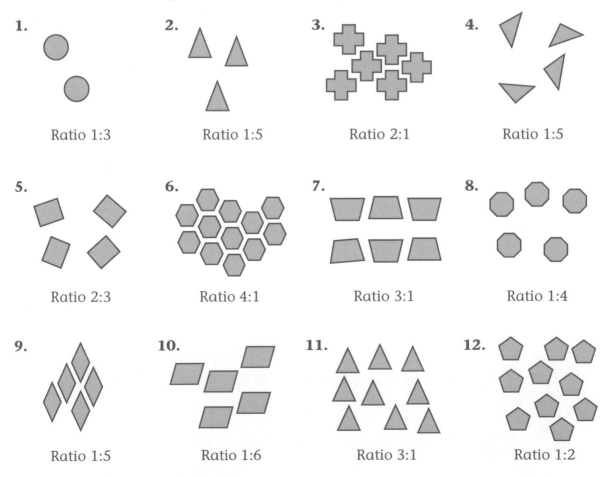

1. Ratio 1:3

2. Ratio 1:5

3. Ratio 2:1

4. Ratio 1:5

5. Ratio 2:3

6. Ratio 4:1

7. Ratio 3:1

8. Ratio 1:4

9. Ratio 1:5

10. Ratio 1:6

11. Ratio 3:1

12. Ratio 1:2

TASK 1   **1.** Measure the heights and bases of each of these 3 triangles and write them down as a ratio **base : height**.

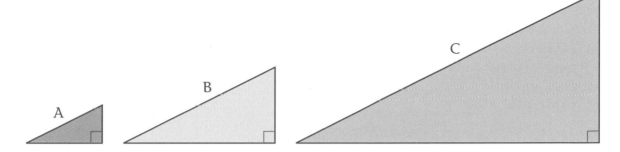

2. Look at each of the ratios. What is the pattern in the ratio?

3. Measure the bases and heights of the triangles below to find which of them have the same ratio as the ones above.

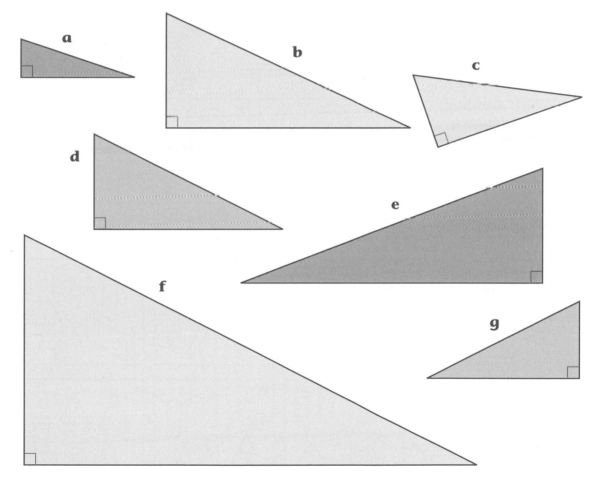

4. A triangle has a base : height ratio of 1 : 2. If its base is 100 cm, what is its height?

5. Another triangle with the same base : height ratio has a base of 15 cm. What is its height?

7 SOLID SHAPES

Key words

cube	cubic
net	solid
volume	length
width	height

This unit will help you to:
→ **identify solid shapes**
→ **understand nets**
→ **find volume**
→ **multiply.**

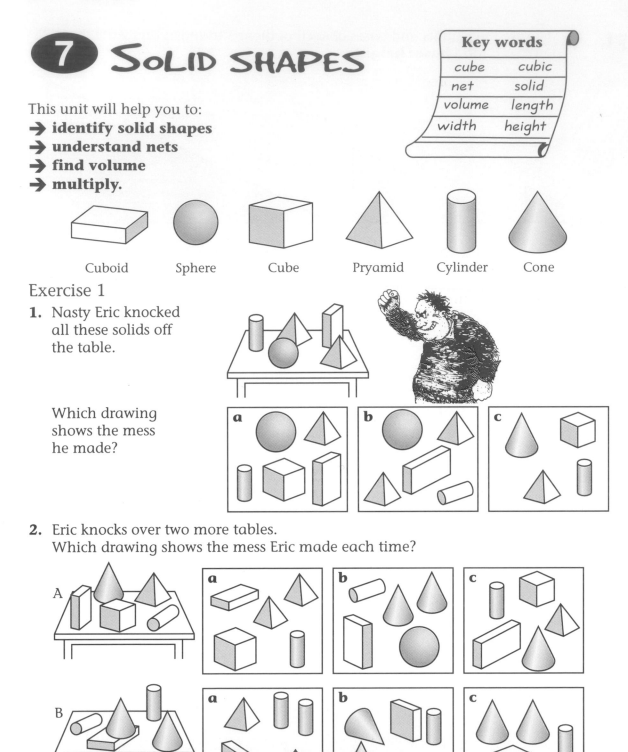

| Cuboid | Sphere | Cube | Pryamid | Cylinder | Cone |

Exercise 1

1. Nasty Eric knocked all these solids off the table.

Which drawing shows the mess he made?

2. Eric knocks over two more tables.
Which drawing shows the mess Eric made each time?

A

B

Exercise 2

How many of these shapes can you see on this page?

1. cubes   **2.** cylinders   **3.** pyramids   **4.** cuboids   **5.** spheres   **6.** cones

NETS

Eric's class have made some shapes out of cardboard.

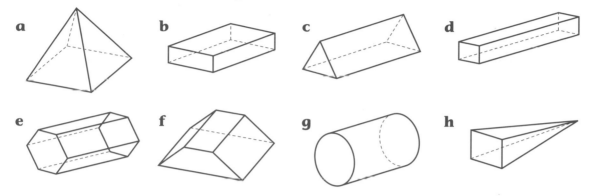

a b c d

e f g h

Exercise 3

Eric is in a bad mood. He pulls apart all the shapes.
When he has unfolded the shapes they look like these below.

Which shape above do you think matches up with the unfolded shape below?

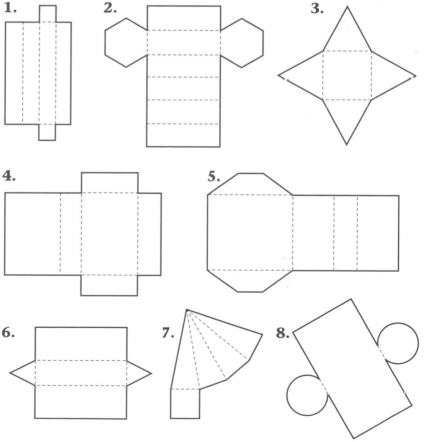

1.

2.

3.

4.

5.

6.

7.

8.

Eric is caught unfolding the shapes by his teacher.
As a punishment the teacher makes Eric draw the
unfolded shapes.
He then makes Eric fold them, and glue them together.

This drawing of an unfolded
shape is called a **net**.

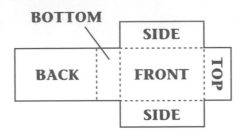

**When the net is folded
it should look like this:**

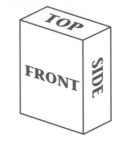

Exercise 4

Here is the net for a cube. Carefully copy it on to card.
Fold the net and glue it to make a solid shape.
Notice that you must leave tabs so that you can glue the edges together.

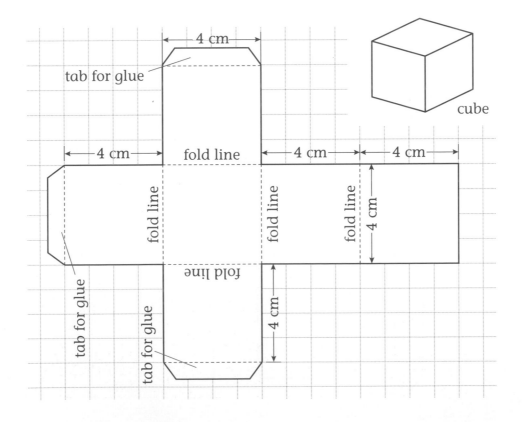

cube

For his homework Eric is told to draw
the net for this shape.

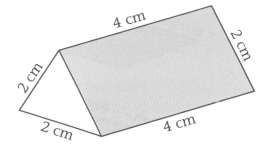

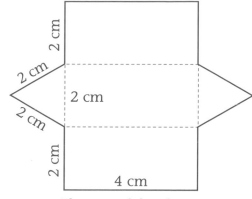

The shape

The net of the shape

Exercise 5

Draw the nets for these shapes.
Draw them full size.

1.

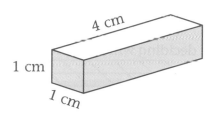

2.

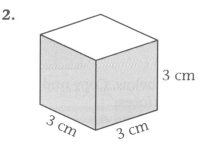

Exercise 6

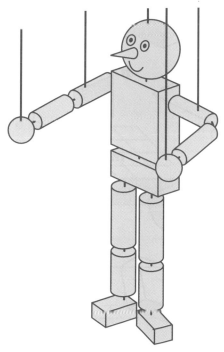

1. How many spheres are there in this puppet?
2. How many cones are there in this puppet?
3. How many cylinders are there in this puppet?
4. How many cuboids are there in this puppet?
5. Which one of the drawings below shows all the
   pieces of the puppet when it is taken apart?

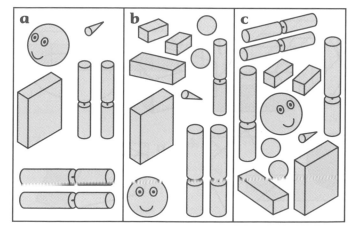

LAYERS AND MULTIPLICATION

Example

Each of these boxes holds 10 cans, (2 rows of 5 cans).

There are 10 cans in each box or layer. You can add to find the total number of cans in the pile:

10 + 10 + 10 + 10 = 40 cans

A quicker way to to multiply:

4 × 10 = 40 cans

Example

These boxes hold 12 cans, (3 rows of 4 cans). You can find the total number of cans by adding:

12 + 12 + 12 + 12 + 12 = 60 cans

There are two different ways to multiply:

5 × 12 cans = 60 cans

or:

5 lots of 10 and 5 lots of 2 = 50 + 10 = 60 cans

Exercise 9

1. You can see there are 10 bags of sugar in the top box
   (2 rows of 5 = 10 bags)
   There are 3 boxes of sugar bags.
   How many bags of sugar are there in all?

2. How many individual items are there in each of the piles of boxes?

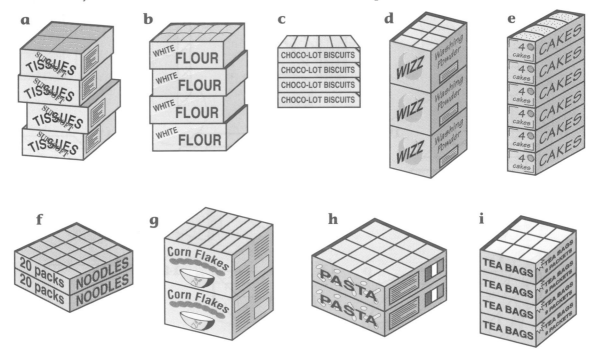

You can find the **volume** of larger shapes without counting cubes.
Find the number of cubes in the top layer, and multiply this by the number of layers.

Example

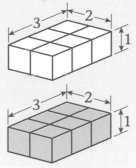

The white layer has a volume of 6 cubes.

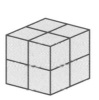

The orange layer has a volume of 6 cubes.

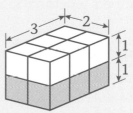

When the two layers are put together they have a volume of 12 cubes.

Exercise 10

Copy and complete the sentences below.

1.

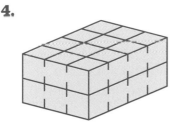

The volume of the block is ___ cubes.

2.

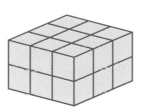

The volume of the block is ___ cubes.

3.

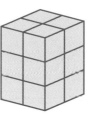

The volume of the block is ___ cubes.

4.

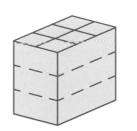

The volume of the block is ___ cubes.

5.

The volume of the block is ___ cubes.

6.

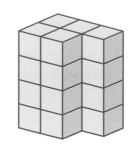

The volume of the block is ___ cubes.

7.

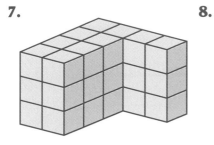

The volume of the block is ___ cubes.

8.

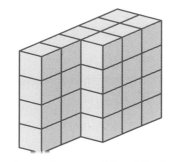

The volume of the block is ___ cubes.

9.

The volume of the block is ___ cubes.

MULTIPLYING

You can **multiply** these three numbers together: 5, 2 and 3.

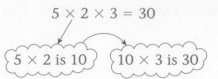

$5 \times 2 \times 3 = 30$

5×2 is 10 10×3 is 30

If you multiply these numbers in a different order, will you get a different answer?

Try: $2 \times 5 \times 3 =$
      $3 \times 2 \times 5 =$
      $2 \times 3 \times 5 =$

Exercise 11

Multiply each group of three numbers together.
Does it matter in which order you multiply the numbers?

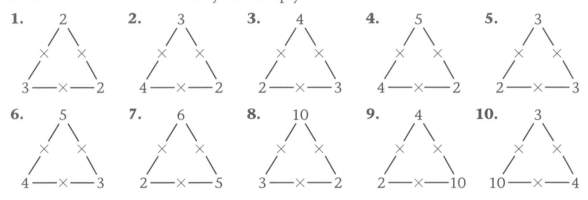

1.   2
   3 —×— 2

2.   3
   4 —×— 2

3.   4
   2 —×— 3

4.   5
   4 —×— 2

5.   3
   2 —×— 3

6.   5
   4 —×— 3

7.   6
   2 —×— 5

8.   10
   3 —×— 2

9.   4
   2 —×— 10

10.   3
   10 —×— 4

Exercise 12

What numbers are missing from each of these multiplication problems?

1. $2 \times 3 \times ? = 24$ **2.** $5 \times 2 \times ? = 50$ **3.** $? \times 4 \times 5 = 40$

4. $3 \times ? \times 2 = 18$ **5.** $? \times 10 \times 2 = 40$ **6.** $3 \times ? \times 3 = 45$

Example

If you wanted to make 18 by multiplying three numbers, you might use 3,3 and 2:
      $3 \times 3 \times 2 = 18$
or $2 \times 3 \times 3 = 18$
or $3 \times 2 \times 3 = 18$

Exercise 13

Make the following numbers by multiplying three figures taken from the group in the ring below.

You can use each figure more than once.

1. 12   **2.** 24   **3.** 30   **4.** 40

5. 60   **6.** 32   **7.** 45   **8.** 48

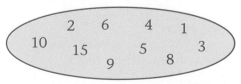

2   6   4   1
10
15   5
   9   8   3

CALCULATING VOLUME

Standard cubes

To measure small volumes we use a **centimetre cube** (written **1 cm³**), as the standard unit. The drawing shows a 1 centimetre cube.
It is 1 cm **long**, 1 cm **wide** and 1 cm **high**.

To find the volume of a solid box you multiply **length**, by **width**, by **height**.

Example

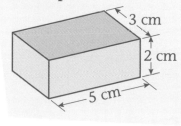

Volume = $l \times w \times h$
This cuboid is 5 cm in length,
              3 cm in width and
              2 cm in height.
The volume of this cuboid is $5 \times 3 \times 2$
= 30 centimetre cubes.
We can write 30 centimetre cubes as 30 cm³.

The ³ shows there are 3 dimensions.

Remember: The formula for finding volume of a box is $l \times w \times h$.

Exercise 14

Find the volume of these objects, and complete the sentences below.

1.

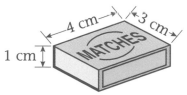

The volume of the box is
4 cm × 3 cm × 1 cm.
The volume is ___ cm³.

2.

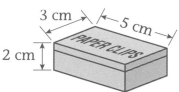

The volume of the box is
3 cm × 5 cm × 2 cm.
The volume is ___ cm³.

3.

The volume of the box is
2 cm × 4 cm × 5 cm.
The volume is ___ cm³.

4.

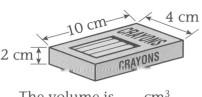

The volume is ___ cm³.

5.

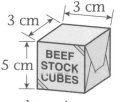

The volume is ___ cm³.

6.

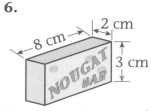

The volume is ___ cm³.

Exercise 15

Find the volume of each block. The shapes are not drawn to scale.

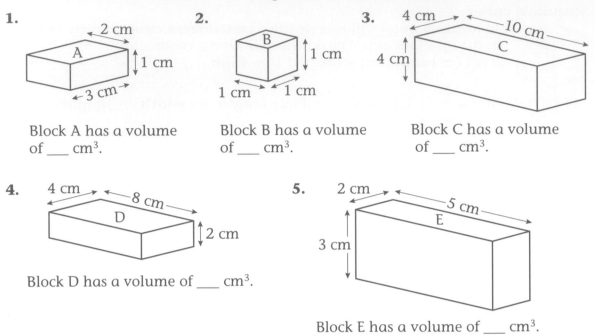

1.

2 cm

A

1 cm

3 cm

Block A has a volume
of ___ cm³.

2.

B

1 cm

1 cm   1 cm

Block B has a volume
of ___ cm³.

3.

4 cm   10 cm

C

4 cm

Block C has a volume
of ___ cm³.

4.   4 cm   8 cm

D

2 cm

Block D has a volume of ___ cm³.

5.   2 cm   5 cm

E

3 cm

Block E has a volume of ___ cm³.

Exercise 16

Find the volume of these shapes. Each shape is made up from the blocks above.

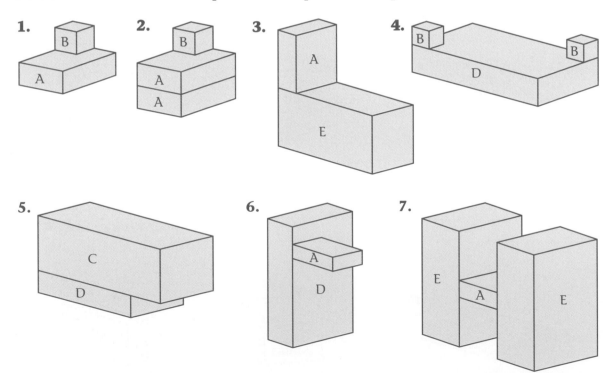

1.
B
A

2.
B
A
A

3.
A
E

4.
B
D
B

5.
C
D

6.
A
D

7.
E
A
E

Example

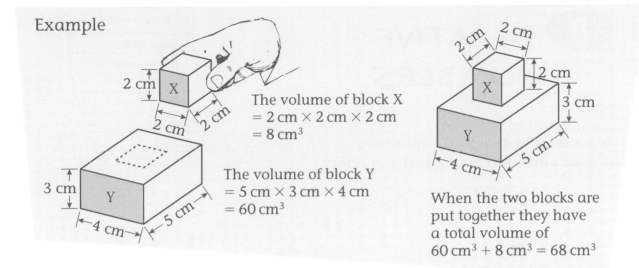

The volume of block X
= 2 cm × 2 cm × 2 cm
= 8 cm³

The volume of block Y
= 5 cm × 3 cm × 4 cm
= 60 cm³

When the two blocks are
put together they have
a total volume of
60 cm³ + 8 cm³ = 68 cm³

Exercise 17

Each shape below is made from more than one block. The dotted lines show where
the blocks are joined. Find the total volume of each shape.

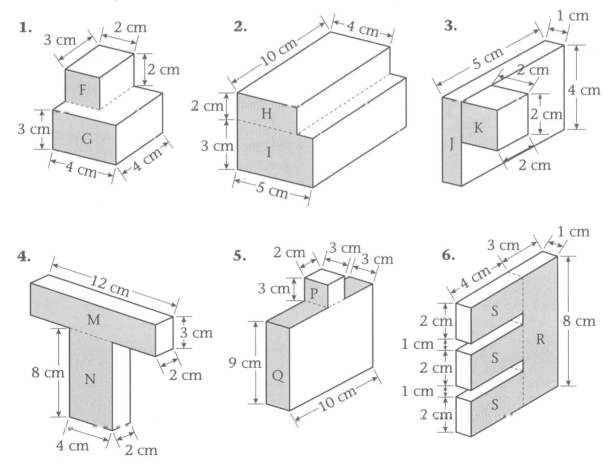

8 NEGATIVE NUMBERS

This unit will help you to:
→ **understand negative numbers**
→ **add and subtract negative numbers.**

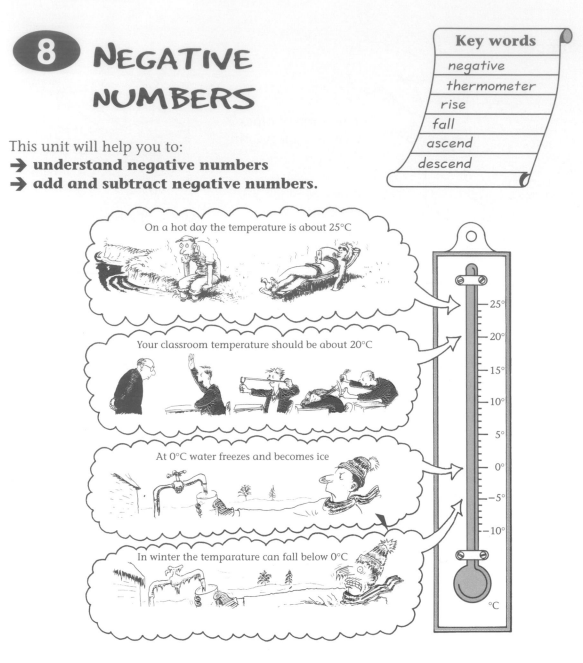

On a hot day the temperature is about 25°C

Your classroom temperature should be about 20°C

At 0°C water freezes and becomes ice

In winter the temperature can fall below 0°C

Exercise 1

Use the picture of the thermometer to help you to answer these questions.

1. a Which of these temperatures is below zero, or freezing point?
   1°C, ⁻5°C, 18°C, ⁻4°C, 7°C, 14°C, ⁻7°C, 17°C, 25°C, ⁻32°C, ⁻1°C
   b Which is the coolest temperature?

2. Rewrite these temperatures in order. Start with the coolest first.
   a 8°C, ⁻6°C, 0°C   **b** ⁻5°C, 7°C, ⁻2°C
   c 14°C, ⁻15°C, 3°C ⁻10°C   **d** 0°C, 2°C, ⁻1°C, 4°C
   e ⁻5°C, ⁻7°C, 2°C   **f** 16°C, ⁻15°C, ⁻6°C
   g ⁻1°C, ⁻8°C, 7°C ⁻10°C   **h** ⁻6°C, 12°C, ⁻11°C

ADDING NEGATIVE NUMBERS

Example

The temperature starts at ⁻1°C
and it rises by 5°.
It finishes at 4°C.

A **rise** in temperature is like **'adding'** heat.

You write the addition like this:

$$^-1 + 5 = 4$$

rise another 4°, **finish** at 4° ⟶ 4°

3°

+4   2°

+5

1°

rise 1° to 0° ⟶ 0°

+1

start at ⁻1° ⟶ ⁻1°

Exercise 2

Copy these and complete the calculations.

1. ⁻3 + 9 =   2. ⁻2 + 7 =   3. ⁻1 + 8 =   4. ⁻4 + 4 =
5. ⁻4 + 5 =   6. ⁻1 + 6 =   7. ⁻6 + 5 =   8. ⁻7 + 2 =
9. ⁻5 + 9 =   10. ⁻1 + 1 =   11. ⁻4 + 6 =   12. ⁻9 + 9 =
13. ⁻3 + 6 =   14. ⁻5 + 3 =   15. ⁻6 + 8 =   16. ⁻5 + 2 =

Exercise 3

1. Calculate the finishing temperatures in this table.
   Use the thermometer to help you.

Starting temperature	Rise in temperature	Finishing temperature
0°	7°	___°
⁻2°	3°	___°
⁻9°	10°	___°
⁻7°	9°	___°
⁻11°	14°	___°
⁻10°	15°	___°
⁻12°	15°	___°
⁻8°	10°	___°
⁻9°	16°	___°
⁻6°	15°	___°

2. **a** If the temperature started at ⁻4°C and finished at 2°C,
      what was the rise?
   b At breakfast the temperature was ⁻6°C, by lunchtime it was 5°C.
      What was the temperature rise?
   c Make up your own 'temperature rise' problem with a rise of 7°C
      (start below zero degrees).

SUBTRACTING NUMBERS

Example

The temperature starts at 5°C and it falls by 7°. It finishes at ⁻2°C.

A **fall** in temperature is like '**taking away or subtracting**' heat.

You write the subtraction like this:

$$5 - 7 = {}^-2$$

start at 5°⟶ 5°
4°
3°
−5   2°   −7
1°
fall 5° to 0°⟶ 0°
−2   ⁻1°
fall another 2°, **finish** at ⁻2°⟶ ⁻2°

Exercise 4

Copy these and complete the calculations.

1. $0 - 3 =$ **2.** $1 - 3 =$ **3.** $4 - 6 =$ **4.** $4 - 5 =$

5. $6 - 8 =$ **6.** $3 - 3 =$ **7.** $2 - 7 =$ **8.** $6 - 10 =$

9. $5 - 12 =$ **10.** $4 - 9 =$ **11.** $5 - 9 =$ **12.** $3 - 15 =$

Notice that the starting points below are all negative numbers, so they all start below zero.

13. ${}^-2 - 3 =$ **14.** ${}^-5 - 3 =$ **15.** ${}^-5 - 6 =$ **16.** ${}^-1 - 8 =$

17. ${}^-8 - 2 =$ **18.** ${}^-3 - 12 =$ **19.** ${}^-5 - 10 =$ **20.** ${}^-11 - 3 =$

Exercise 5

1. Calculate the finishing temperatures in this table.
Use the thermometer to help you.

Starting temperature	Fall in temperature	Finishing temperature
0°	9°	____°
⁻2°	3°	____°
9°	10°	____°
⁻7°	9°	____°
11°	14°	____°
10°	5°	____°
⁻12°	15°	____°
⁻8°	10°	____°

°C
10
9
8
7
6
5
4
3
2
1
0
−1
−2
−3
−4
−5
−6
−7
−8
−9
−10
−11
−12
−13
−14
−15
−16
−17
−18
−19
−20

2. a A diver is 4 m below the surface level. If she descends another 24 m how far under the surface will she be now?

  b If she now rises 7 m, write her new depth as a negative number.

  c Sempa died in 10AD. He was 26 years old. In which year BC was he born?

COORDINATES

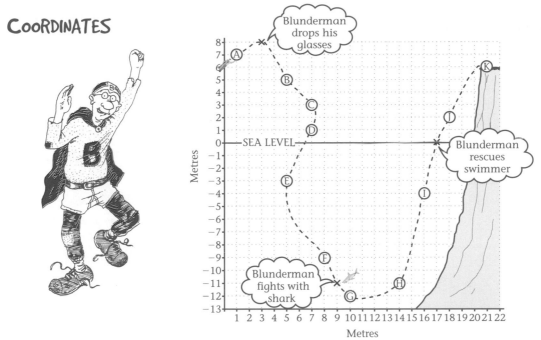

Exercise 6

Blunderman can fly through the air and under water.
He starts his journey at point A.

1. How high above sea level is Blunderman at point A?
2. How high above sea level is he when he drops his glasses?
3. How many metres does he **descend** between points B and C?
4. How far below sea level is he at point E?
5. How far below sea level did Blunderman fight the shark?
6. How far below sea level is he at point G?
7. What letter will you find at a depth of ⁻9 m?
8. How many metres does he **ascend** between points H and K?
9. How many metres does he **ascend** between points G and J?
10. How many metres does he **descend** between points B and F?

Exercise 7

1. Give coordinates for the following points:
   a B   **b** E   **c** G   **d** I
2. What happens at these coordinates?
   a (3, 8)   **b** (9, ⁻11)   **c** (17, 0)
3. Give the coordinates for point K.
4. Between coordinates (1, 7) and (3, 8) does Blunderman **ascend** or **descend**?
5. Between coordinates (7, 3) and (10, ⁻12) does he **ascend** or **descend**?
6. Blunderman moves from (5, 5) to (5, ⁻3).
   a Has he **ascended** or **descended**?
   b How many metres has he moved **vertically**?

9 FRACTIONS

This unit will help you to:
→ **divide to find fractions of amounts.**

Key words
half
quarter
third
fifth
of

HALVES, $\frac{1}{2}$

The pupils at Dimwig Hall School are in for some bad news.
Due to a shortage of money, Dr Dimwig, the Head has to
make cutbacks.

Before the cutbacks the pupils' food plates looked like this:

a 2 sausages
4 tomatoes
2 eggs

b 4 potatoes
2 carrots
4 fish fingers
6 sprouts

c 2 drum sticks
6 mushrooms
8 chips
12 peas

d 10 chocolate digestives
8 chocolate fingers
12 almonds

Example

To find half of a number, divide by 2.
To find half of 8 you divide 8 by 2.   **8 ÷ 2 = 4**

Exercise 1

1. Redraw or write out what would be on the plates when the food rations have been
   cut by half.

2. Other school equipment is reduced by half.
   How many items will be left after their number has been halved?

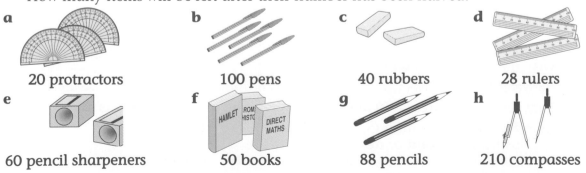

a
20 protractors

b
100 pens

c
40 rubbers

d
28 rulers

e
60 pencil sharpeners

f
50 books

g
88 pencils

h
210 compasses

QUARTERS, $\frac{1}{4}$

At Dimwig Hall all classes are divided into four House Groups.

There are 12 pupils in class 9G

So there are 3 pupils in each House.
To find $\frac{1}{4}$ of a number you divide by 4.
$\frac{1}{4}$ of 12 = 12 ÷ 4 = 3

Exercise 2

Look at the drawings below and say how many pupils will belong in each House.
Remember there are four Houses, so you divide by four.

1.   **2.**   **3.**   **4.**

Class 1M   Class 2R   Class 3H   Class 4P

5. There are 28 students in 11F. How many will be in each House Group?

6. There are 40 students in 10G. How many will be in each House Group?

7. There are 80 students in Year 11. How many will be in each House Group?

8. There are 800 students in the school. How many will be in each House Group?

Exercise 3

Calculate $\frac{1}{4}$ of the number of crosses in the boxes below.

1.   **2.**   **3.**   **4.**   **5.**

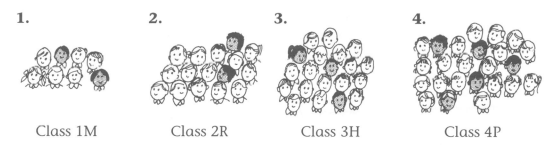

Answer these questions. The first has been done for you.

6. $\frac{1}{4}$ of 12 = 3   **7.** $\frac{1}{4}$ of 8 = ☐   **8.** $\frac{1}{4}$ of 20 = ☐

9. $\frac{1}{4}$ of 16 = ☐   **10.** $\frac{1}{4}$ of 32 = ☐   **11.** $\frac{1}{4}$ of 44 = ☐

12. $\frac{1}{4}$ of 36 = ☐   **13.** $\frac{1}{4}$ of 48 = ☐   **14.** $\frac{1}{4}$ of 100 = ☐

FINDING $\frac{3}{4}$ OF AMOUNTS

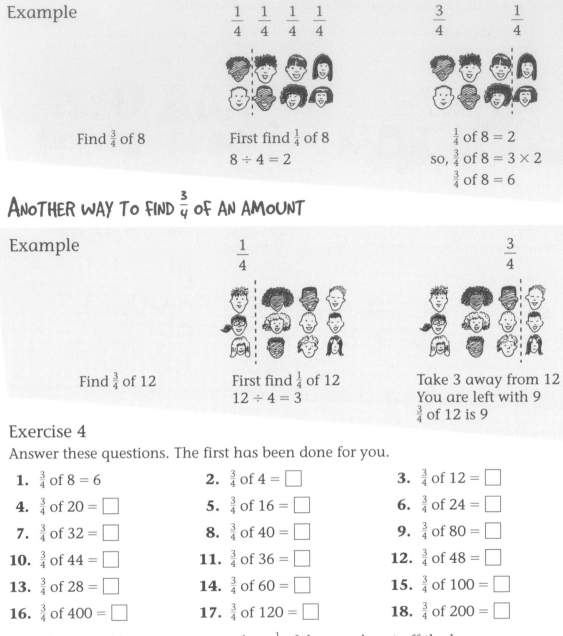

Example

$\frac{1}{4}$ $\frac{1}{4}$ $\frac{1}{4}$ $\frac{1}{4}$ $\frac{3}{4}$ $\frac{1}{4}$

Find $\frac{3}{4}$ of 8

First find $\frac{1}{4}$ of 8
$8 \div 4 = 2$

$\frac{1}{4}$ of 8 = 2
so, $\frac{3}{4}$ of 8 = 3 × 2
$\frac{3}{4}$ of 8 = 6

ANOTHER WAY TO FIND $\frac{3}{4}$ OF AN AMOUNT

Example

$\frac{1}{4}$ $\frac{3}{4}$

Find $\frac{3}{4}$ of 12

First find $\frac{1}{4}$ of 12
$12 \div 4 = 3$

Take 3 away from 12
You are left with 9
$\frac{3}{4}$ of 12 is 9

Exercise 4

Answer these questions. The first has been done for you.

1. $\frac{3}{4}$ of 8 = 6
2. $\frac{3}{4}$ of 4 = ☐
3. $\frac{3}{4}$ of 12 = ☐
4. $\frac{3}{4}$ of 20 = ☐
5. $\frac{3}{4}$ of 16 = ☐
6. $\frac{3}{4}$ of 24 = ☐
7. $\frac{3}{4}$ of 32 = ☐
8. $\frac{3}{4}$ of 40 = ☐
9. $\frac{3}{4}$ of 80 = ☐
10. $\frac{3}{4}$ of 44 = ☐
11. $\frac{3}{4}$ of 36 = ☐
12. $\frac{3}{4}$ of 48 = ☐
13. $\frac{3}{4}$ of 28 = ☐
14. $\frac{3}{4}$ of 60 = ☐
15. $\frac{3}{4}$ of 100 = ☐
16. $\frac{3}{4}$ of 400 = ☐
17. $\frac{3}{4}$ of 120 = ☐
18. $\frac{3}{4}$ of 200 = ☐

19. There are 32 passengers on a bus. $\frac{1}{4}$ of the people get off the bus.
    How many are left on the bus?

20. There are 24 blue and red tiles in a pattern. $\frac{1}{4}$ of the tiles are blue.
    How many red tiles are there?

21. There are 52 plates in a crate. When the crate is opened $\frac{3}{4}$ of the plates are found
    to be broken. What number of plates are left intact?

22. A 440 m length of road is being repaired. After one day the workers have
    repaired $\frac{3}{4}$ of the road. What length of road is left unrepaired?

FRACTIONS OF LARGER NUMBERS

Example

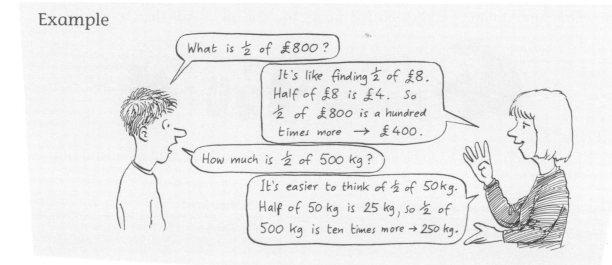

What is ½ of £800?

It's like finding ½ of £8. Half of £8 is £4. So ½ of £800 is a hundred times more → £400.

How much is ½ of 500 kg?

It's easier to think of ½ of 50 kg. Half of 50 kg is 25 kg, so ½ of 500 kg is ten times more → 250 kg.

Exercise 5
Find half of these numbers.

1. Half of £6 =

2. Half of £60 =

3. ½ of £600 =

4. ½ of £4 =

5. Half of £40 =

6. ½ of £400 −

7. ½ of £30 =

8. Half of £300 =

9. Half of £3000 =

10. Half of £10 =

11. ½ of £100 =

12. Half of £1000 =

Example

To find a quarter of £120, imagine you are finding a quarter of £12 → £3, then multiply the £3 by ten.

¼ of £12 is £3

So, ¼ of £120 is 10 × £3 → £30.

Exercise 6
Find quarters of these numbers.

1. Quarter of £8 =

2. Quarter of £80 =

3. Quarter of £800 =

4. ¼ of £16 −

5. ¼ of £160 =

6. ¼ of £1600 =

7. ¼ of £4 =

8. ¼ of £40 =

9. ¼ of £400 =

10. Quarter of £10 =

11. Quarter of £100 =

12. Quarter of £1000 =

THIRDS, $\frac{1}{3}$

The students at Dimwig Hall have been told they must give $\frac{1}{3}$ of their pocket money to the school fund. To find $\frac{1}{3}$ of their pocket money the students divide their money by 3.

Exercise 7

Copy and complete the table below showing how much each student gave and how much they kept.

Name	Pocket money	$\frac{1}{3}$ of pocket money	Money kept
Martin	£15	£5	£10
Ali	£9		
Betty	£18		
Rachid	£21		
Ray	£3		
Derek	£30		
Arun	£6		
Keran	£12		
Dinish	£33		
Rosie	£45		

Exercise 8

Answer these questions. The first has been done for you.

1. $\frac{1}{3}$ of 9 = 3
2. $\frac{1}{3}$ of 3 = ☐
3. $\frac{1}{3}$ of 30 = ☐
4. $\frac{1}{3}$ of 15 = ☐
5. $\frac{1}{3}$ of 12 = ☐
6. $\frac{1}{3}$ of 18 = ☐
7. $\frac{1}{3}$ of 60 = ☐
8. $\frac{1}{3}$ of 300 = ☐
9. $\frac{1}{3}$ of 150 = ☐

Example

To find $\frac{2}{3}$ you can divide by 3 and multiply by 2

£9

$\frac{1}{3}$ of £9 = £3

$\frac{2}{3}$ of £9 = £6

Exercise 9

Answer these questions. The first has been done for you.

1. $\frac{2}{3}$ of 9 = 6
2. $\frac{2}{3}$ of 12 = ☐
3. $\frac{2}{3}$ of 15 = ☐
4. $\frac{2}{3}$ of 30 = ☐
5. $\frac{2}{3}$ of 18 = ☐
6. $\frac{2}{3}$ of 24 = ☐
7. $\frac{2}{3}$ of 36 = ☐
8. $\frac{2}{3}$ of 21 = ☐
9. $\frac{2}{3}$ of 33 = ☐
10. $\frac{2}{3}$ of 90 = ☐
11. $\frac{2}{3}$ of 300 = ☐
12. $\frac{2}{3}$ of 120 = ☐

FIFTHS, $\frac{1}{5}$

Good news at Dimwig Hall!
Dr Dimwig has decided that holidays will be increased by $\frac{1}{5}$.

To find $\frac{1}{5}$ of an amount
you divide it by 5.

$\frac{1}{5}$ of 10 is $10 \div 5 = \underline{2}$

Exercise 10

Answer these questions. The first has been done for you.

1. $\frac{1}{5}$ of 10 = 2   **2.** $\frac{1}{5}$ of 20 = ☐   **3.** $\frac{1}{5}$ of 5 = ☐

4. $\frac{1}{5}$ of 15 = ☐   **5.** $\frac{1}{5}$ of 25 = ☐   **6.** $\frac{1}{5}$ of 35 = ☐

7. $\frac{1}{5}$ of 50 = ☐   **8.** $\frac{1}{5}$ of 60 = ☐   **9.** $\frac{1}{5}$ of 40 = ☐

10. $\frac{1}{5}$ of 55 = ☐   **11.** $\frac{1}{5}$ of 100 = ☐   **12.** $\frac{1}{5}$ of 150 = ☐

Exercise 11

The table below shows the length of school holidays at Dimwig Hall.

a   Find $\frac{1}{5}$ of each holiday in days.
b   Increase each holiday by $\frac{1}{5}$.
c   Copy and complete the table.

Holidays	Summer	Autumn	Christmas	Spring	Easter	Whitsun
Number of days	35	5	20	10	15	5
$\frac{1}{5}$ increase in days	*	*	*	2	*	1
New number of days in each holiday	*	*	*	12	*	6

FRACTIONS OF AMOUNTS

Example

To find $\frac{3}{5}$ of 10
we start by finding $\frac{1}{5}$ $\frac{1}{5}$ of 10 = $10 \div 5 = 2$ $\frac{3}{5}$ of 10 = $3 \times 2 = 6$

Exercise 12

1. Calculate $\frac{3}{5}$ of these amounts.
    a 10   **b** 15   **c** 20   **d** 30   **e** 50   **f** 150

2. Calculate $\frac{2}{5}$ of the amounts above.

3. Calculate $\frac{4}{5}$ of the amounts above.

Exercise 13

Neesha has drawn a plan of a draughts board.

Neesha begins by marking out the squares on the board.
The edge of the board is 40 cm long.
Neesha needs to make 8 divisions.
Each division will be $\frac{1}{8}$ of 40 cm.

a What is $\frac{1}{8}$ of 40 cm?

Neesha has a piece of wood that is 168 cm long.
She must cut it into four equal lengths.
Each length will be $\frac{1}{4}$ of 168 cm.

b What is $\frac{1}{4}$ of 168 cm?

Neesha needs to paint the squares on the board.
There are 64 squares.
She will paint $\frac{1}{2}$ of these squares black.

c What is $\frac{1}{2}$ of 64 squares?.

Next Neesha will make the draughts pieces.
She will cut them from a thick dowel rod.
Each piece of dowel rod is 20 cm long.
Neesha will divide each rod into 8 equal pieces.

d What is $\frac{1}{8}$ of 20 cm?
e How many rods will Neesha need to make 32 pieces?

20 cm

Neesha has finished making 32 draught pieces.
She decides to paint $\frac{1}{2}$ of them red.

f What is $\frac{1}{2}$ of 32?

Exercise 14

Complete these sentences.

1.

$\frac{1}{5}$ of the money in the wallet can
be seen. The wallet has £___ in it.

2.

$\frac{1}{4}$ of the train can be seen.
Altogether the train has ___ coaches.

3.

You can see $\frac{2}{5}$ of the
biscuits.
Altogether the box
holds ___ biscuits.

4.

The box holds 40 matches.
The fraction taken from
the box is ___.

5.

The fraction of the pile
that is missing is ___.

6.

You can see $\frac{2}{5}$ of the
windows of the tower.
The tower has ____
windows altogether.

7.

$\frac{3}{4}$ of the books on the shelf
are shown. There should
be ___ books altogether.

8.

$\frac{3}{4}$ of the cakes have been
eaten. There were ___ cakes
before any were eaten.

Exercise 15

Answer these questions.

1. Pat has spent $\frac{2}{3}$ of her money. She started with £18. How much is left?

2. How much is $\frac{2}{5}$ of £1.50?

3. How much is $\frac{2}{3}$ of 300 kg?

4. How many years are there in $\frac{4}{5}$ of a century?

5. How many minutes are there in $\frac{2}{3}$ of 2 hours?

10 DECIMALS

This unit will help you to:
→ **recall the decimal system**
→ **read decimal dials**
→ **do calculations involving decimals (×, ÷)**
→ **round off decimals.**

Key words
increase
decrease
difference

REVISION

Exercise 1

What decimal part of each rod is

a shaded   **b** **not** shaded?

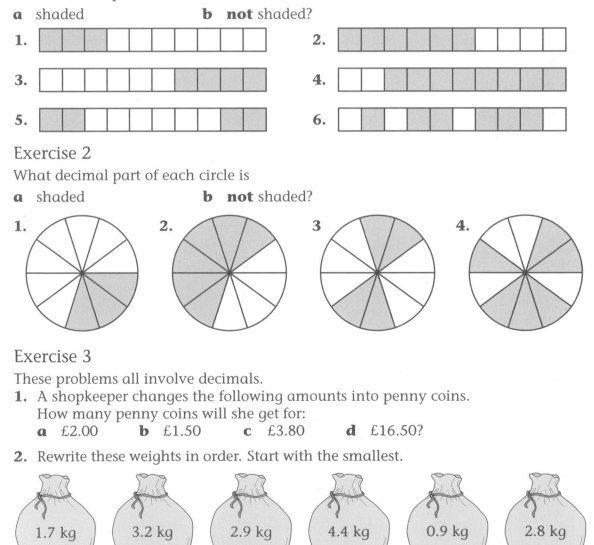

Exercise 2

What decimal part of each circle is

a shaded   **b** **not** shaded?

Exercise 3

These problems all involve decimals.

1. A shopkeeper changes the following amounts into penny coins.
   How many penny coins will she get for:
   a £2.00   **b** £1.50   **c** £3.80   **d** £16.50?

2. Rewrite these weights in order. Start with the smallest.

1.7 kg   3.2 kg   2.9 kg   4.4 kg   0.9 kg   2.8 kg

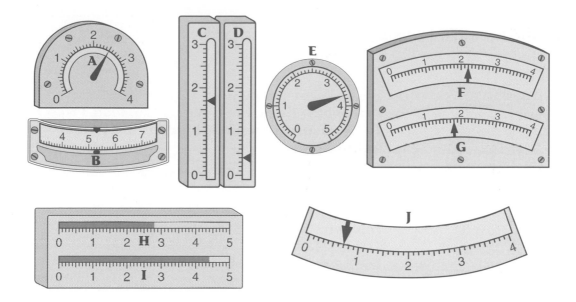

Exercise 4

Read the dials above to answer these questions.

1. Which dial reads 3.7?   2. Which dial reads 2.5?
3. Which dial reads 0.7?   4. Which dial reads 4.4?
5. Which dial reads 2.8?   6. Which dial reads 1.8?
7. Which dial reads 2.2?   8. Which dial reads 5.3?
9. Which dial reads 0.4?   10. Which dial reads 1.7?

Exercise 5

Write down the new readings when these changes happen.

1. Dial A is **increased** by 1.0   2. Dial J is **increased** by 2.0
3. Dial D is **increased** by 2.0   4. Dial B is **decreased** by 1.0
5. Dial C is **decreased** by 0.5   6. Dial H is **increased** by 0.2
7. Dial I is **increased** by 0.4   8. Dial A is **decreased** by 0.3
9. Dial A is **decreased** by 1.5   10. Dial G is **increased** by 0.8

Exercise 6

1. Which dials show readings that are less than 1?
2. Find pairs of dials that have a **difference** of exactly 1.
3. Arrange the dial readings in order from the smallest to the largest.
4. On the dial below, reading B is double reading A. Each division on the dial is 0.1 units.
   Write down the numbers A and B. Use the number line to help you.

A   B

ESTIMATING WITH DECIMALS

Example

The parcel weighs between 1 kg and 2 kg.
Its weight is 1.7 kg. It is closer to 2 kg, than 1 kg.
To the nearest whole kilogram the parcel weighs 2 kg.

This parcel weighs 2.3 kg. The weight is closer to 2 kg than 3 kg.
To the nearest whole kilogram, the parcel weighs 2 kg.

Exercise 7

Write down each of these decimal measurements to the nearest whole number.

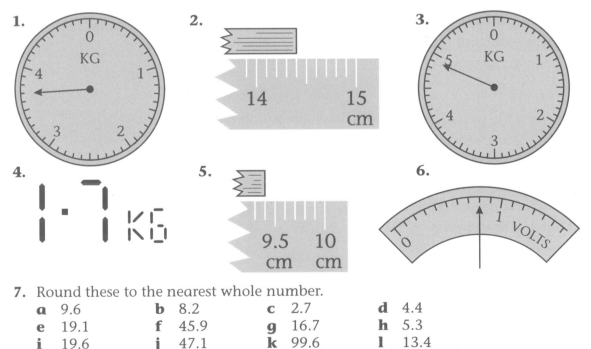

1.

2.   14   15 cm

3.

4.   1.7 KG

5.   9.5   10 cm   cm

6.   0   1 VOLTS

7. Round these to the nearest whole number.
    a 9.6   **b** 8.2   **c** 2.7   **d** 4.4
    e 19.1   **f** 45.9   **g** 16.7   **h** 5.3
    i 19.6   **j** 47.1   **k** 99.6   **l** 13.4

8. This number has been rounded to the nearest whole one. List some of the numbers that it could have been before it was rounded.

20

USING ESTIMATION WITH ADDITION

It is difficult to add the weights of these parcels in your head, because there are too many numbers and decimal points to remember.

You can give a close estimation of the addition by rounding off the decimal weights before you add.

Like this: $1.3 + 2.1 + 5.8 + 3.2 + 4.1 + 4.4 + 5.8 + 9.9$
$$\downarrow \quad \downarrow \quad \downarrow \quad \downarrow \quad \downarrow \quad \downarrow \quad \downarrow \quad \downarrow$$
$$1 + 2 + 6 + 3 + 4 + 4 + 6 + 10 \approx 36 \text{ kg}$$

This sign means is about the same as

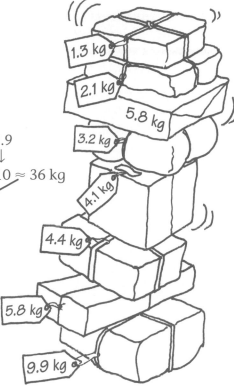

Exercise 8

Use rounding off, to estimate the answers to these additions and subtractions.

1. $2.7 + 3.8 + 6.2 + 5.4 + 6.1 \approx$
2. $0.8 + 2.6 + 10.4 + 0.4 + 2.9 + 1.5 \approx$
3. $2.6 + 3.8 + 0.5 + 8.4 \approx$
4. $5.8 + 0.6 - 2.3 \approx$
5. $10.8 + 1.1 + 10.4 + 0.5 - 2.9 \approx$
6. $5.0 + 2.1 + 7.7 + 0.6 + 0.9 - 8.3 \approx$
7. $12.6 - 10.4 - 1.7 \approx$
8. $24.9 - 10.5 + 0.7 \approx$
9. Think of some decimal numbers that will fit into these estimated additions. Do not use whole numbers.
   a $\quad 2.3 + 5.9 + \square \approx 10$ b $\quad 10.6 + 1.8 + 1.5 + \square \approx 20$

ACCURATE DECIMAL ADDITION AND SUBTRACTION

When you need to make accurate additions or subtractions, you can set out the calculations like this.

$$2.9 + 6.8 + 13.4 + 5 \rightarrow$$

Notice that the 5 is written as 5.0 and all the decimal points are underneath each other.

```
   2.9
   6.8
  13.4
+  5.0
 ─────
  28.1
```

Exercise 9

a Estimate the answers to these.
b Calculate the answers accurately.

1. $5.2 + 6.9 + 0.6$
2. $4.0 + 2.7 + 4.5 + 3 + 4.7$
3. $9.9 + 0.1 + 5.2 + 0.6$
4. $0.8 + 0.3 + 0.7 + 0.8 + 2$
5. $15.0 - 2.1$
6. $72.3 - 25.1$
7. $9.0 + 7.3$
8. $5.0 + 2.1 + 7.7 + 0.6 + 0.9 - 8.3$

For each card
a estimate answers to the questions
b calculate the answers accurately.

Practice card 1

1. 2.1 + 4.2 + 3.5   **2.** 3.2 + 0.4 + 3.2

3. 1.5 + 0.2 + 7.1   **4.** 2.7 + 3.0 + 2.2

5. 4.0 + 3.3 + 1.6   **6.** 3.1 + 0.5 + 4.1

7. 8.1 + 0.4 + 1.3   **8.** 0.2 + 2.3 + 4.3

9. 5.1 + 1.4 + 0.3   **10.** 0.2 + 0.5 + 0.3

Practice card 2

1. 7.1 + 0.9   **2.** 6.4 + 0.8 + 1

3. 3.5 + 4.4 + 2.4   **4.** 0.2 + 8.5 + 1.5

5. 3.0 + 5.8 + 0.5   **6.** 7.0 + 1.8 + 0.6

7. 6.2 + 1.2 + 1.7   **8.** 8.1 + 0.4 + 0.9

9. 6.6 + 2.6   **10.** 3.2 + 3.4 + 1.9

Practice card 3

1. 4.1 + 4.2 + 3.4   **2.** 9.4 + 4.0

3. 5.4 + 4.1 + 3.3   **4.** 0.2 + 7.5 + 6.3

5. 12.1 + 9.2   **6.** 6.0 + 7.2 + 8.7

7. 8.1 + 0.5 + 9.3   **8.** 6.1 + 8.7

9. 2.0 + 8.3 + 3.6   **10.** 13.2 + 9.2

Practice card 4

1. 7.1 + 4.6 + 2.4   **2.** 8.8 + 2.1 + 5.3

3. 6.9 + 6.9   **4.** 9.2 + 0.7 + 3.1

5. 5.1 + 1.3 + 2.4   **6.** 2.2 + 2.8 + 8.9

7. 8.8 + 7.2   **8.** 0.9 + 4.9 + 5.0

9. 7 + 2.5 + 0.5   **10.** 3.0 + 5.8 + 8.3

Practice card 5

1. 5.8 − 4.2   **2.** 9.5 − 4.3

3. 6.4 − 2.0   **4.** 7.7 − 7.5

5. 8.5 − 5.1   **6.** 6.8 − 3.0

7. 7.6 − 0.4   **8.** 2.5 − 0.1

9. 8.8 − 4.5   **10.** 13.1 − 9.0

Practice card 6

1. 15.8 − 4.9   **2.** 9.5 − 4.7

3. 4.4 − 0.7   **4.** 7.1 − 3.9

5. 3.3 − 2.4   **6.** 6.8 − 3.9

7. 8.1 − 4.7   **8.** 7.4 − 0.9

9. 2.4 − 1.5   **10.** 6.1 − 3.7

Exercise 10

Straw A is 3.9 cm, straw B is 6.4 cm, straw C is 10.3 cm, straw D is 8.5 cm.

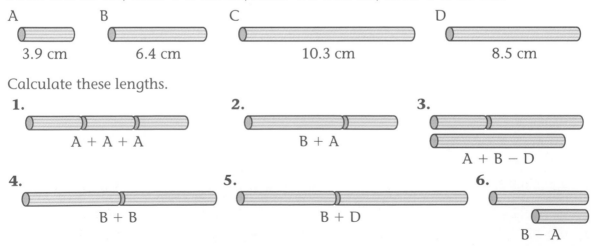

A   B   C   D

3.9 cm   6.4 cm   10.3 cm   8.5 cm

Calculate these lengths.

1.
A + A + A

2.
B + A

3.
A + B − D

4.
B + B

5.
B + D

6.
B − A

MULTIPLYING DECIMAL NUMBERS

This timber wolf measures about 1.5 m long.

← 1.5 m →

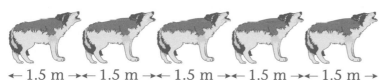

← 1.5 m →← 1.5 m →← 1.5 m →← 1.5 m →← 1.5 m →

Nose to tail, 5 of these wolves would measure:
1.5 m + 1.5 m + 1.5 m + 1.5 m + 1.5 m
You can do this calculation in your head or on paper.

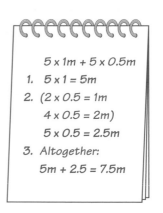

5 x 1m + 5 x 0.5m
1. 5 x 1 = 5m
2. (2 x 0.5 = 1m
   4 x 0.5 = 2m)
   5 x 0.5 = 2.5m
3. Altogether:
   5m + 2.5 = 7.5m

Exercise 11

Multiply these lengths (in your head or making notes like those above).

1. 5×4.5 m =   **2.** 4×6.5 m =   **3.** 3×3.5 m =   **4.** 6×2.5 m =

5. 8×2.5 m =   **6.** 3×5.5 m =   **7.** 6×3.5 m =   **8.** 3×7.5 m =

OTHER WAYS TO MULTIPLY DECIMALS

These video cassettes are 2.3 cm deep.

$\frac{\perp}{\top}$ 2.3 cm

The height of this pile of cassettes can be calculated in different ways.
Here are two different ways:

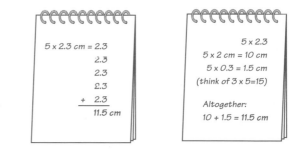

5 x 2.3 cm = 2.3
              2.3
              2.3
              2.3
          +   2.3
            11.5 cm

5 x 2.3
5 x 2 cm = 10 cm
5 x 0.3 = 1.5 cm
(think of 3 x 5=15)

Altogether:
10 + 1.5 = 11.5 cm

Exercise 12

Find the height of each pile of video cassettes. Use your own method.

1.

3 cassettes

2.
6 cassettes

3.
2 cassettes

4.
4 cassettes

5.

7 cassettes

6.

8 cassettes

7.
9 cassettes

8.
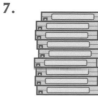
10 cassettes

USING ESTIMATION TO MULTIPLY DECIMALS

Which ever way you multiply decimals, you can estimate an answer that you can expect.
This is a good way to check your working.

Like this: 5·3 × 6.

5·3 is close to 5 and 5 × 6 is 30, so you should expect an answer a little more than 30.

5.3 × 6
  5 × 6 = 30
  5 × 0.3 = 1.5

so,
5.3 × 6 = 31.5

Exercise 13

Give estimates for these decimal multiplications.

1. 3.3×6 is about ......
2. 4.1×9 is about ......
3. 10.4×7 is about ......
4. 15.1×3 is about ......
5. 12.1×5 is about ......
6. 9.5×5 is about ......

Sometimes you need to estimate upwards: 5·9 × 3.
5·9 is close to 6, and 6 × 3 is 18.
So the answer should be a little less than 18.

Exercise 14

Decide which is the best way to estimate these multiplications.

1. 3.9×5 is about ......
2. 5.8×5 is about ......
3. 2.7×7 is about ......
4. 3.3×3 is about ......
5. 9.2×3 is about ......
6. 9.9×8 is about ......
7. 7.6×5 is about ......
8. 4.1×9 is about ......
9. 10.8×3 is about ......
10. 6.6×4 is about ......
11. 9.4×5 is about ......
12. 9.5×5 is about ......

a Estimate answers to these.
b Calculate the answers.

Practice card 1	
1. $5.3 \times 4 =$	**2.** $4.2 \times 3 =$
3. $3.4 \times 3 =$	**4.** $5.1 \times 3 =$
5. $7.3 \times 2 =$	**6.** $2.6 \times 4 =$
7. $8.4 \times 2 =$	**8.** $1.2 \times 9 =$
9. $6.0 \times 5 =$	**10.** $5.5 \times 3 =$
11. $2.4 \times 4 =$	**12.** $2.1 \times 8 =$

Practice card 2	
1. $2.5 \times 5 =$	**2.** $7.1 \times 8 =$
3. $6.2 \times 3 =$	**4.** $5.6 \times 4 =$
5. $7.9 \times 3 =$	**6.** $7.2 \times 6 =$
7. $6.8 \times 5 =$	**8.** $10.8 \times 2 =$
9. $7.5 \times 5 =$	**10.** $2.8 \times 6 =$
11. $5.3 \times 4 =$	**12.** $4.2 \times 3 =$

MULTIPLYING DECIMAL NUMBERS BY TEN

When you multiply a decimal number by 10, you move the digits along one place to the left.

Remember the abacus. The value of each spike is ten times larger than the spike to the right.

To multiply 1.6 by 10, move the beads to the next spike to the left.

So $1.6 \times 10 = 16$

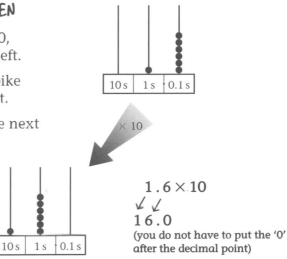

1.6×10
16.0
(you do not have to put the '0' after the decimal point)

Exercise 15

Multiply these decimal numbers by ten.

1. $2.5 \times 10 =$	**2.** $3.6 \times 10 =$	**3.** $7.3 \times 10 =$
4. $4.9 \times 10 =$	**5.** $5.7 \times 10 =$	**6.** $9.4 \times 10 =$
7. $3.6 \times 10 =$	**8.** $7.8 \times 10 =$	**9.** $5.4 \times 10 =$
10. $6.8 \times 10 =$	**11.** $9.9 \times 10 =$	**12.** $12.4 \times 10 =$

Exercise 16

Answer these problems involving multiplying by ten.

1. A bag of compost weighs 6.5 kg. How much will ten bags weigh?

2. One filing cabinet is 45.6 cm wide. If there are ten cabinets in a row, will they fit into a space 463 cm wide?

3. Drinking straws are 10.8 cm long. End to end, how long will ten straws measure?

4. A van travels 12.7 km on 1 litre of fuel. How far will it travel on 10 litres?

DIVIDING DECIMAL NUMBERS BY TEN

When you **multiply** a decimal number by 10, you move the digits one place to the **left**.   So 10 x 2·8 = 28. An estimate would be 10x3, which is 30.

When you **divide** a decimal number by 10, you move the digits one place to the **right** So 28 ÷ 10 = 2·8. Look at the abacus to see it happen !

Exercise 17

Divide these decimal numbers by ten.

1. 65 ÷ 10 =   **2.** 53 ÷ 10 =   **3.** 74 ÷ 10 =   **4.** 34 ÷ 10 =

5. 56 ÷ 10 =   **6.** 31 ÷ 10 =   **7.** 89 ÷ 10 =   **8.** 90 ÷ 10 =

9. 30 ÷ 10 =   **10.** 58 ÷ 10 =   **11.** 72 ÷ 10 =   **12.** 92 ÷ 10 =

Exercise 18

These pieces of string have been divided into 10 sections.
Estimate, then calculate, the length of one section in each question.

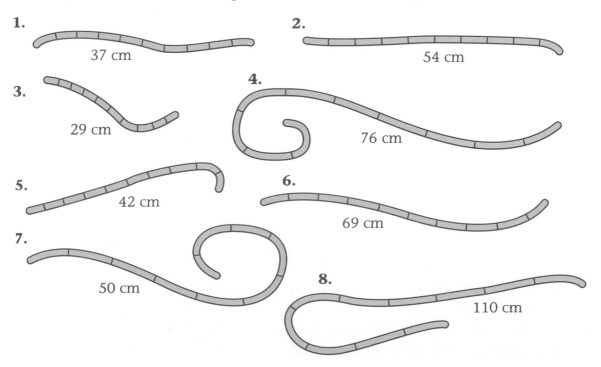

1. 37 cm

2. 54 cm

3. 29 cm

4. 76 cm

5. 42 cm

6. 69 cm

7. 50 cm

8. 110 cm

DIVIDING BY NUMBERS OTHER THAN TEN

To share £4.50 between three of you, start by sharing the £4.

This gives £1 each, with £1 left over.   Now there is £1.50 left to share.

£1.50 divided into three parts is £0.50, or 50p each.

Altogether then, you get £1.50 each.

Exercise 19

Work out these division problems.

1. At the Chewo sweet factory, Mary has to pack 19.2 kg of sweets into 6 boxes. How many kg will she put into each box?

2. At the Fizzpop drinks factory, Tom has to put 22.5 litres of shandy into 5 jars. How many litres will he put into each jar?

3. At the Lux lace factory, Robin has to cut 7.8 metres of ribbon into 6 equal lengths. How long will each piece be?

4. There are 4 boxes of fruit on this weighing scale. How much does each box weigh?

5. Five workers in an office win £26.55 between them in a raffle. How much do they each receive?

REVIEW 1

A. SOLIDS

1. Sort these solids into the correct rings. The first one is done for you.

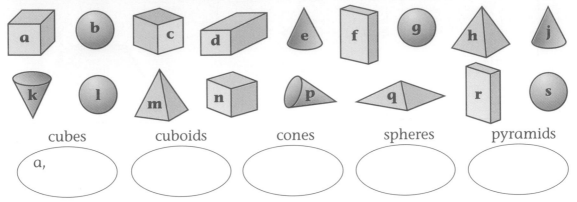

cubes   cuboids   cones   spheres   pyramids

a,

2. What solid shapes will these nets produce when folded?

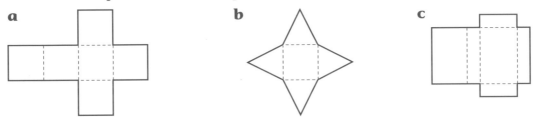

a   **b**   **c**

B. VOLUME

1. a How many centimetre cubes would it take to construct this shape?
   b What is the volume of this shape?

2. a How many centimetre cubes would it take to construct this shape?
   b What is the volume of this shape?

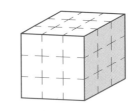

3. What are the volumes of these shapes?

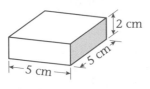

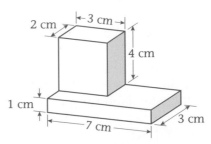

C. ANGLES IN A CIRCLE

1. There are ____° in a circle.

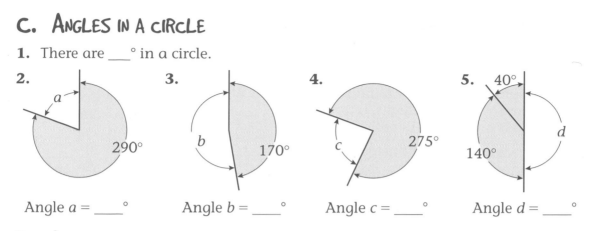

2.
a
290°

3.
b
170°

4.
c
275°

5. 40°
d
140°

Angle a = ____°   Angle b = ____°   Angle c = ____°   Angle d = ____°

D. ANGLES AND PARALLEL LINES

By comparing the angles in each diagram below, say which drawings show a pair of parallel lines.

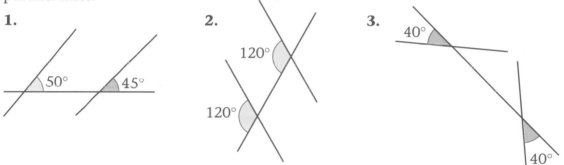

1.
50°   45°

2.
120°
120°

3.
40°
40°

E. FRACTIONS

1. From a group of 12 people, 6 cycle to work. What fraction cycle to work?

2. Roger saved £15. He spent £5 of this. What fraction did he spend?

3. If 9 pupils go home to lunch, 7 pupils have a packed lunch, and 5 pupils have lunch in a local café, what fraction of these pupils have a packed lunch?

4. Rewrite these fractions in order of size, from largest to smallest.
   a $\frac{1}{5}, \frac{1}{2}, \frac{1}{4}$ **b** $\frac{1}{10}, \frac{1}{3}, \frac{2}{3}$ **c** $\frac{1}{4}, \frac{1}{2}, \frac{1}{10}, \frac{3}{4}$

F. DECIMALS

1. If one bag of rice weighs 1.2 kg, how much will 4 bags weigh?

2. If one bag of flour weighs 1.5 kg, how much will 5 bags weigh?

3. If 5.2 kg of soil is shared between 2 flower pots, how much is put into each pot?

4. If a bucket can carry 4 kg of sand, how many buckets can be filled from 9.6 kg of sand?

THINKING PUZZLE

The table opposite is a multiplication table, but which one?

1. Use the information below to find which table it is! The letters stand for the digits, 0 to 9. The table is not written in order.

2. Write down the clues that helped you the most.

3. Choose another of the multiplication tables and make your own puzzle. Try it on your teacher or a friend.

The 'p' times table
$g \times p = mk$
$a \times p = kw$
$k \times p = e$
$w \times p = km$
$mj \times p = pj$
$m \times p = p$
$e \times p = ms$
$s \times p = kg$
$c \times p = mc$
$p \times p = a$

H. NEGATIVE NUMBERS

1. Copy the number line below.

$$-9 \ -8 \ -7 \ -6 \ -5 \ -4 \ -3 \ -2 \ -1 \ 0 \ 1 \ 2 \ 3 \ 4 \ 5 \ 6 \ 7 \ 8 \ 9$$

G   D   F   A   B   C   E

2. Write down the positions of the letters A to G.

3. Add arrows and letters to your number line showing: H at ($^-$1) and K at ($^-$5).

4. Calculate or count the distance between these points on the number line:
   a A and B   **b** A and E   **c** B and E   **d** A and F
   e F and D   **f** F and G   **g** B and F   **h** D and C

5. Copy and complete these calculations. Use the number line to help.
   a $7 - 6 =$ **b** $6 - 7 =$ **c** $5 - 8 =$
   d $^-2 + 4 =$ **e** $^-7 + 4 =$ **f** $^-9 + 9 =$
   g $^-8 + 10 =$ **h** $^-2 - 2 =$ **i** $^-4 + \square = 1$

I. DECIMAL MEASUREMENT

1. What is the length of each of these lines?

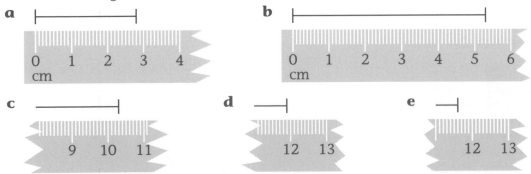

2. Add 1.6 cm to each of the measurements above.
3. Take 2.3 cm from each of the measurements above.

 11 CIRCLES

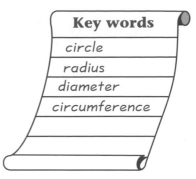

Key words

circle
radius
diameter
circumference

This unit will help you to:
→ **use a pair of compasses accurately**
→ **understand fractions of circles**
→ **understand the connection between diameter, radius and the circumference of circles.**

MAKING CIRCLES

The goat is eating the grass. When its chain becomes tight, the goat cannot go any further and it has to move around.

What is the shape that the goat has made by eating the grass?

When the chain is kept tight, could the goat make any other shape?

TASK 1   Using a ruler and pencil trace the path of the goat.

1. Put a fine pencil mark in the centre of your page. Label if C for centre.

2. Make another mark 3 cm away from the centre mark and label it M.

3. Make at least another 20 marks like M.
   Making more marks will give you a better drawing.

4. Join up the marks to make a smooth curve.
   The shape that you have made should be a circle.

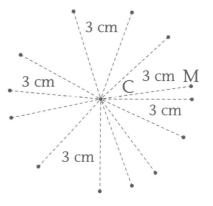

TASK 2

1. Repeat Task 1 with a mark 5 cm away from the centre. Try to improve your circle.

2. Copy the sentence below and fill in the missing words:
   'A circle is a path that is always the same .... from the .... point.'

DIAMETER, RADIUS AND CIRCUMFERENCE

Learn the names of these distances in circles.

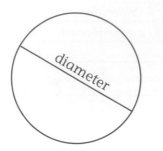 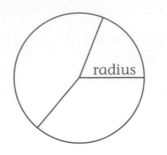 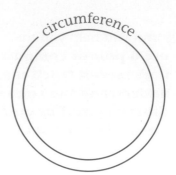

The **diameter** is the distance across the circle from edge to edge. The diameter goes through the centre.

The **radius** is the distance from the centre to the edge of the circle.

The **circumference** is the distance around the edge of the circle.

Exercise 1

Use your ruler to measure these distances on the circle opposite. Copy and complete the statements.

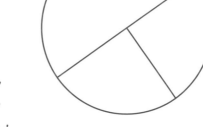

1. The distance of the diameter of the circle is .... cm.

2. The distance of the radius is .... cm.

3. Which two of these statements are true?

    Copy out the correct statements.
    a 'The diameter is half the distance of the radius.'
    b 'The radius is half the distance of the diameter.'
    c 'The diameter is twice the distance of the radius.'
    d 'The radius is twice the distance of the diameter.'

4. These circles are not drawn to size. Use what you learned above to find the missing distances of these circles.

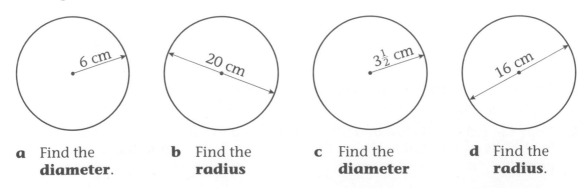

a Find the **diameter**.

b Find the **radius**

c Find the **diameter**

d Find the **radius**.

Puzzles with diameter and radius

Remember: The diameter is twice the distance of the radius.
The radius is half the distance of the diameter.

Example
How long is the red line?

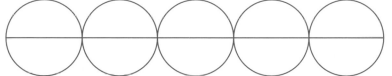

The diameter of each of these circles is the same. Each one is 10 cm long. The red line must be 4 × 10 cm long. The red line is 40 cm long.

Exercise 2

Use the idea above to solve these problems.

1. Calculate the length of the red line.
The circles all have a diameter of 8 cm.

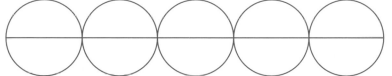

2. The radius of each of these circles is 3 cm. What is the length of the red line?

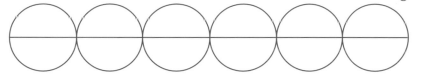

3. The two circles are the same size. The red line is 60 cm long.

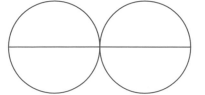

    a What is the diameter of each circle?
    b What is the radius?

4. The radius of each circle is 5 cm.
    a How many circles will fit into each row?
    b How many rows of circles will fit into the box?
    c How many circles will fit into the box altogether?

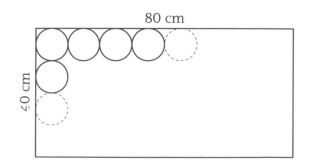

CIRCUMFERENCE OF CIRCLES

You can see that the circumference of the circle below is bigger than its diameter.

TASK 3 **1.** Do you think that the circumference is about

    a half as big as the diameter
    b three times as big as the diameter
    c ten times as big as the diameter
    d one hundred times as big as the diameter?

2. Write down your estimate into your book.

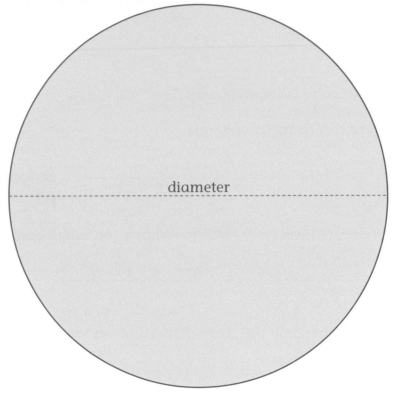

diameter

3. Check your estimate to the question above.
    You will need: a ruler, about 40 cm of string.
    a Carefully wind the string around the circumference. Keep the string tight. Do not let it become 'kinked'.
    b When you have stretched the string around the circumference exactly once, mark the string with your pen.
    c Put the string tightly against your ruler, and measure the length of the circumference. Your answer should be about 30 cm.
    d Use your ruler to measure the diameter. It will be 10 cm.

4. **a** Divide your estimate for the circumference by the length of the diameter. Your answer should be about 3.
    b Copy and complete this sentence:
    'The circumference of the circle is about .... times the diameter.'

CIRCUMFERENCE IS ABOUT 3 × DIAMETER

Example

The diameter of this wheel is 20 cm.
You know that its circumference is about 3 times
the diameter.

So the circumference of the wheel is about 3 × 20 cm.
The circumference is about 60 cm.

You cannot say that the circumference **is** 60 cm, because
your answer is only an **estimation**.

Exercise 3

Use 'circumference is about 3 × diameter', to estimate
the circumference of the circles in these drawings.

1. Estimate the circumference of the mug.

   Circumference is about 3 × .... cm.
   Circumference is about .... cm.

   10 cm

2. The diameter of the CD is 12 cm.
   What is the circumference of the CD?

   Circumference is about 3 × .... cm.
   Circumference is about .... cm.

   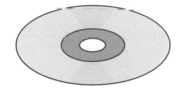

3. The diameter of the plate is 30 cm.
   What is the circumference of the plate?

   Circumference is about 3 × .... cm.
   Circumference is about .... cm.

4. The diameter of the Big Wheel is 100 m.
   What is its circumference?

   Circumference is about 3 × .... m.
   Circumference is about .... m.

12 ALGEBRA

Key words

formula
balance
equation
perimeter

This unit will help you to:
→ **work with symbols**
→ **solve simple balancing problems and equations**
→ **make and use basic formulas.**

USING LETTERS

Example

Here are three tins of peas.
If you call each tin *b*, you can describe
this group as 3*b*.

Exercise 1

Describe each of these groups using letters.

1.

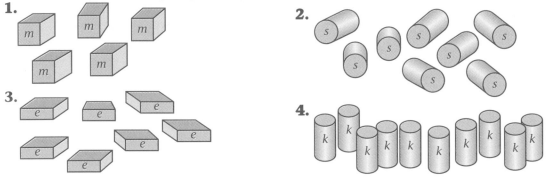

2.

3.

4.

Exercise 2

Find the weight of each can. The first is done for you.

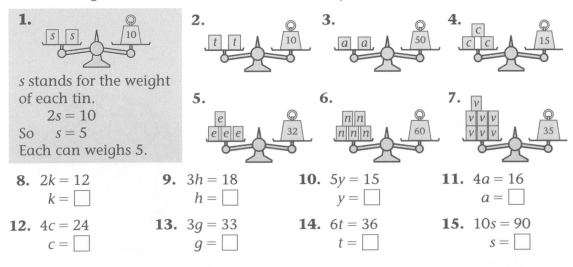

1.

s stands for the weight
of each tin.
    2*s* = 10
So   *s* = 5
Each can weighs 5.

2.

3.

4.

5.

6.

7.

8. 2*k* = 12
    k = ☐

9. 3*h* = 18
    h = ☐

10. 5*y* = 15
    y = ☐

11. 4*a* = 16
    a = ☐

12. 4*c* = 24
    c = ☐

13. 3*g* = 33
    g = ☐

14. 6*t* = 36
    t = ☐

15. 10*s* = 90
    s = ☐

SOLVING EQUATIONS

Exercise 3

Find the weight of each bottle. The first is done for you.

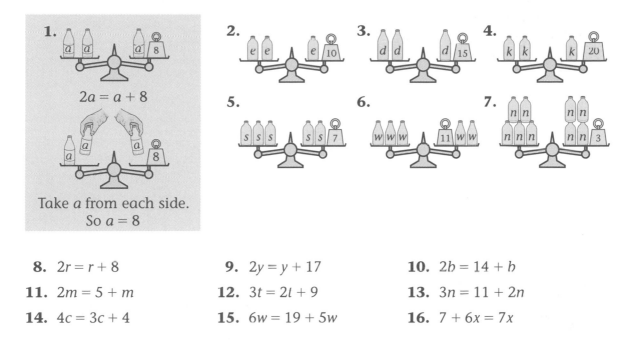

1.

$2a = a + 8$

Take a from each side.
So $a = 8$

8. $2r = r + 8$

9. $2y = y + 17$

10. $2b = 14 + b$

11. $2m = 5 + m$

12. $3t = 2l + 9$

13. $3n = 11 + 2n$

14. $4c = 3c + 4$

15. $6w = 19 + 5w$

16. $7 + 6x = 7x$

Exercise 4

Find the weight of each parcel. The first is done for you.

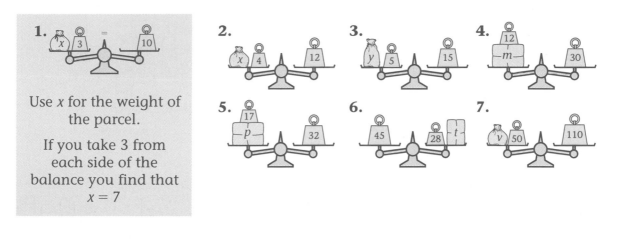

1.

Use x for the weight of the parcel.

If you take 3 from each side of the balance you find that $x = 7$

8. $r + 8 = 10$

9. $f + 5 = 9$

10. $w + 11 = 20$

11. $k + 10 = 17$

12. $a + 25 = 30$

13. $n + 9 = 23$

14. $34 = c + 4$

15. $54 = 20 + w$

16. $47 = 19 + x$

Exercise 5

Using what you know about algebra, work out how many cans there are in each box.
Write an equation to represent each drawing. Use b to stand for the number of cans
in a box.
The first is done for you.

1.

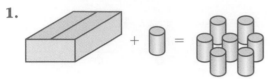

$$b + 1 = 7$$
(remove one can from each side)
$$b = 6$$

2.

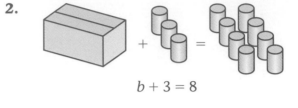

$$b + 3 = 8$$

3.

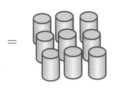

4.

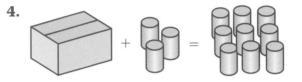

5.

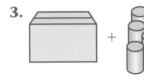

6.

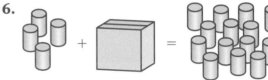

7.

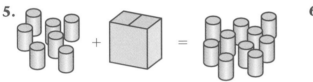

$$2b + 7 = 3b$$
(remove two boxes from each side)
$$b = 7$$

8.

$$2b + 12 = 4b$$

9.

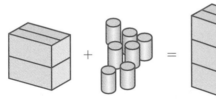

10.

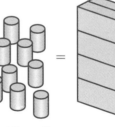

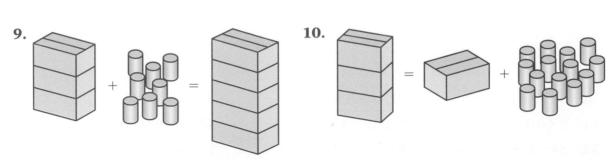

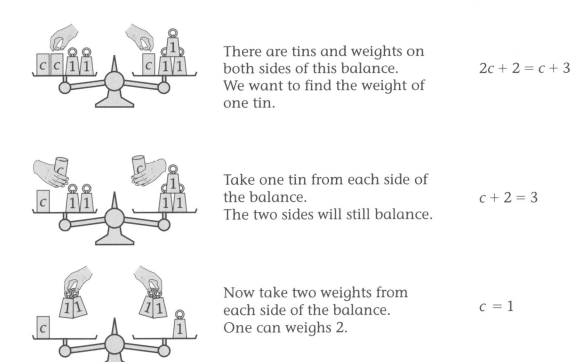

There are tins and weights on both sides of this balance. We want to find the weight of one tin.

$2c + 2 = c + 3$

Take one tin from each side of the balance. The two sides will still balance.

$c + 2 = 3$

Now take two weights from each side of the balance. One can weighs 2.

$c = 1$

Exercise 6
Calculate the weight of each can in these questions.

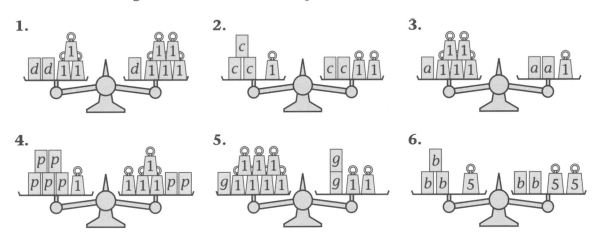

Exercise 7
Find the value of the letters in each equation.

1. $3c + 2 = 2c + 7$ 2. $3p + 6 = 2p + 10$ 3. $5t + 8 = 4t + 12$

4. $4f + 6 = 3f + 7$ 5. $7a + 2 = 6a + 9$ 6. $9v + 10 = 8v + 15$

7. $8r + 12 = 7r + 18$ 8. $10q + 10 = 9q + 17$ 9. $2e + 10 = 18 + e$

MAKING SIMPLE FORMULAS

You can use letters to make simple formulas for the perimeters of shapes.
Example

Remember: Perimeter means the distance around the edges of a shape.

Example

Use p to stand for the perimeter of the triangle. In this triangle the sides are all the same length.
They are all a units long.

The formula for the perimeter is:
$$p = a + a + a$$
$$p = 3a$$

Exercise 8

Make simple formulas for the perimeters of these shapes.
Use p to stand for perimeter. Start like this: $p = \ldots$
In each shape all sides are the same length.

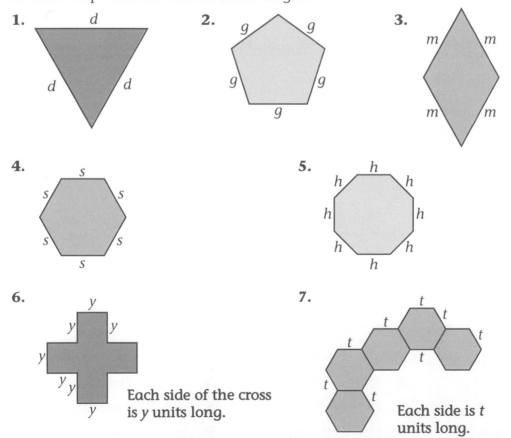

1. d

2. g g g g g

3. m m m m

4. s s s s s s

5. h h h h h h h

6. y

Each side of the cross is y units long.

7. t

Each side is t units long.

USING MORE THAN ONE SYMBOL

Example 1

The long sides of the rectangle are *f* units long,
the short sides are *g* units long.

The perimeter is $g + g + f + f$ or $2g + 2f$
$$p = 2g + 2f$$

Exercise 9

Give a formula for the perimeter of each shape.

1.

n   *t*

n

2.

h

b   *b*

h

3.

v   *t*

x

4.

10

a   *a*

a   *a*

10

5.

5.5

b   *2b*

5.5

6.

5   *e*   3

e   *e*

f   *f*

t   *t*

e

7. The perimeter of the cross is 36 cm.
All sides are equal in length.
How long is each side?

Jenny is the wages clerk for the Clogworth Fashion factory.
She has to work out the wages for each of the workers.

Each worker gets a **basic wage** of £140, and a **bonus** of
£5 for each dress they make.

So, if a worker makes 6 dresses in a week, their bonus will be:

$$(6 \times £5) = £30$$ bonus

Exercise 10

Workers make the following number of dresses.
Calculate the bonus they will each earn.
Remember that they receive £5 bonus for each dress made.

1. Rita: 5 dresses   2. Carl: 10 dresses   3. Niham: 7 dresses
4. Wayne: 12 dresses   5. Meera: 15 dresses   6. Ray: 20 dresses
                7. Atif: 19 dresses   8. Deana: 25 dresses

Each time Jenny had to calculate a total wage
she would do it like this. It was very awkward.

6 dresses:
6 dresses at £5 each is £30, and £140 basic
wage is a total of £170.

Exercise 11

Using the number of dresses made in Exercise 10,
work out the total wage for each worker.

Jenny found an easier way to do her calculations.

She found a **formula**.

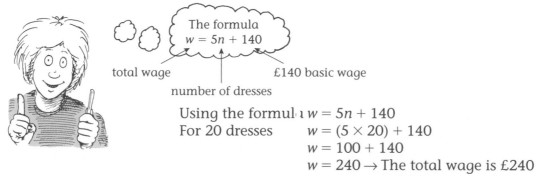

The formula
$w = 5n + 140$

total wage   £140 basic wage
        number of dresses

Using the formula $w = 5n + 140$
For 20 dresses $w = (5 \times 20) + 140$
                  $w = 100 + 140$
                  $w = 240 \rightarrow$ The total wage is £240

Exercise 12

Use the formula $w = 5n + 140$ to work out the wages for these workers.

1. Mavis made 9 dresses   2. Harry made 19 dresses   3. Tom made 11 dresses
4. Leo made 13 dresses   5. Keran made 16 dresses   6. Jan made 21 dresses

The workers are given a pay rise.
They are now paid a bonus of £6 for each dress and a basic wage of £150.

The new formula is $w = 6n + 150$

Exercise 13

Use the formula $w = 6n + 150$ to find the wages when:

1. $n = 2$	**2.** $n = 4$	**3.** $n = 6$	**4.** $n = 1$
5. $n = 3$	**6.** $n = 5$	**7.** $n = 7$	**8.** $n = 10$
9. $n = 12$	**10.** $n = 14$	**11.** $n = 20$	**12.** $n = 21$

The formula for wages is changed again. Now the workers are paid a bonus of £8 per dress and a basic wage of £165.
The new formula is $w = 8n + 165$

Exercise 14

Use the formula $w = 8n + 165$ to find the wages when:

1. $n = 1$	**2.** $n = 3$	**3.** $n = 4$	**4.** $n = 2$
5. $n = 5$	**6.** $n = 6$	**7.** $n = 7$	**8.** $n = 8$
9. $n = 10$	**10.** $n = 9$	**11.** $n = 1\frac{1}{2}$	**12.** $n = 2\frac{1}{2}$

Exercise 15

1. Janice packs dresses into boxes.
Her basic wage is £95 per week, and her bonus is £3 for each box she packs.
   a Write the formula to calculate her total wage.
   b She packs 31 boxes in one week.
      Use the formula to calculate her wages.

> In your answer use w for the total wage and n for the number of boxes packed.

2. Khalid drives the dresses to shops.
His basic wage is £170 per week, and his bonus is £10 for each delivery he makes.
   a Write the formula to calculate his total wage.
   b Khalid makes 12 deliveries in one week.
      Use the formula to calculate his wages.

> In your answer use w for the total wage and n for the number of deliveries.

3. Tulay sells dresses in a shop.
Her basic wage is £88 per week, and her bonus is £2.50 for every dress she sells.
   a Write the formula to calculate her total wage.
   b Tulay sells 10 dresses in one week.
      Use the formula to calculate her wages.

> In your answer use w for the total wage and n for the number of dresses sold.

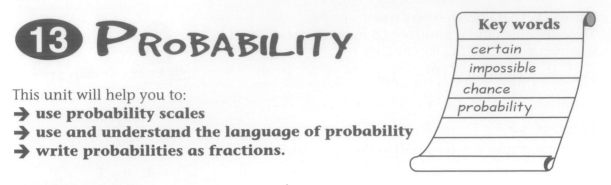

13 PROBABILITY

This unit will help you to:
→ **use probability scales**
→ **use and understand the language of probability**
→ **write probabilities as fractions.**

Key words
certain
impossible
chance
probability

IS IT POSSIBLE?

Below are four sentences. Each sentence has been placed under a heading that describes how 'probable' it is.

certain	high probability	low probability	impossible
It is certain that you have a name.	It is highly probable that you will eat some food in the next 24 hours.	There is a low probability that you will find buried treasure tomorrow.	It is impossible to fly by flapping your hands.

Exercise 1

Copy out a table like the one above. Write in the four headings – 'certain', 'high probability', 'low probability' and 'impossible'.

Put each of the following statements under the heading that you think best describes its probability.

a SOMEONE WILL WRITE YOU A LETTER SOON.

b YOU COULD THROW A FEATHER FROM YOUR CLASSROOM AS FAR AS THE SUN.

c YOU WERE BORN.

d YOU WILL DRINK SOMETHING BEFORE MIDNIGHT TONIGHT.

e A FLOWER WILL GROW OUT OF YOUR BEST FRIEND'S HEAD.

f YOU WILL GET MARRIED.

g YOU ARE LOOKING AT THIS BOOK.

h SOMEWHERE ON EARTH A PERSON IS TALKING.

i YOU WILL WALK ON THE SUN TOMORROW.

j SOMEONE WILL GIVE YOU £1000 THIS WEEK.

k YOU WILL BECOME AN ELEPHANT TRAINER WHEN YOU LEAVE SCHOOL.

l YOU WILL WATCH TELEVISION THIS EVENING.

m You will meet an alien tomorrow.
n The next person you speak to will wear glasses.
o You roll a dice five times and score 6 every time.
p You will see a car sometime in the next 24 hours.

CHANCE

Ken wants to go to the cinema, Ruth wants to go to the funfair.
They decide to flip a coin.
The result can either be 'heads' or 'tails'.
Ken knows that his chances of winning are **one chance out of two** or $\frac{1}{2}$.

Exercise 2

Ruth and Ken go to the funfair. Ken plays 'Find the Pea'.
There are three cups. A pea is hidden under one of them.
Ken's chances of picking the correct cup are:
one chance in three or $\frac{1}{3}$.

1. If there were 5 cups, Ken's chances would be:
one chance in * or $\frac{1}{*}$.

2. If there were 7 cups, Ken's chances would be:
one chance in * or $\frac{1}{*}$.

3. If there were 4 cups, Ken's chances would be:
one chance in * or $\frac{1}{*}$.

4. If there were 20 cups, Ken's chances would be:
one chance in * or $\frac{1}{*}$.

Exercise 3

What are Ruth's chances of winning in each of these games?

1.

Ruth's chances of picking the winning number are $\frac{1}{*}$.

2.
Ruth's chances of picking the winning number are $\frac{1}{*}$.

3. *Find the Ace*

Ruth's chances of picking the ace are $\frac{1}{*}$.

4. **Lucky Numbers**

19	7	22	6	11	32	10
37	17	2	29	3	8	16
4	28	5	18	14	33	25

Ruth's chances of picking the lucky number are $\frac{1}{*}$.

5. *Roulette*
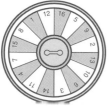
Ruth's chances of picking the winning number are $\frac{1}{*}$.

6.  **RAFFLE TICKET**
Ruth buys a raffle ticket. 150 tickets were sold.
Ruth's chances of having the winning ticket are $\frac{1}{*}$.

7. **Lucky Dip**

One of these packages contains a present.
Ruth's chances of picking the present are $\frac{1}{*}$.

8.
The chances of the swinging arrow landing on the blue section are $\frac{1}{*}$.

Example

If the arrow is spinning on this wheel of fortune, the probability that it lands on the blue section is $\frac{1}{8}$ because there is only one blue section.

The probability of the arrow resting on a blue section on this wheel is $\frac{2}{8}$ because two out of the eight sections are blue. $\frac{2}{8}$ can also be written as $\frac{1}{4}$.

Exercise 4

Find the probability of the arrows stopping on a blue section.
Write your answers as fractions.

1.   **2.**   **3.**   **4.**   **5.**   **6.**   **7.**

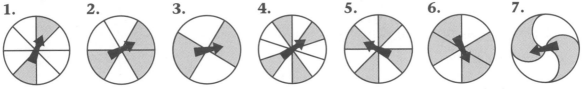

8. Find the probability of the arrow stopping on a white section of each drawing above. Give your answers as fractions.

Exercise 5

There are two 'black' cards in each hand below.
What is the probability of picking a 'black' card?

1.   **2.**   **3.**   **4.**   **5.**   **6.**

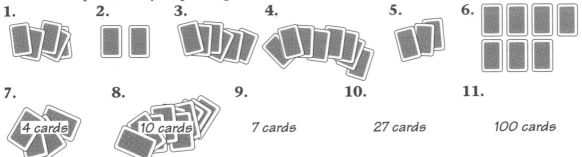

7.   **8.**   **9.**   **10.**   **11.**

4 cards   10 cards   7 cards   27 cards   100 cards

12. Which is the only hand above from which you are certain to pick a 'black' card on the first go?

Exercise 6

Work out the chances of making these scores with a dice.

1. What are the chances of rolling a 'six'?
2. What is the probability of rolling a 'one'?
3. What is the probability of rolling a 'six' or a 'one'?
4. What are the chances of rolling a 'one', 'six' or 'three'?
5. What are the chances of rolling a 'two', 'six', 'five' or 'three'?

PROBABILITY SCALE

You can use a **scale** to show probability. The scale goes from 0 to 1.

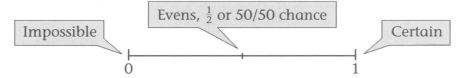

Evens, $\frac{1}{2}$ or 50/50 chance

Impossible

Certain

0   1

Exercise 7

Draw a scale for each of these events.
Mark the scale to show the likely probability of each event.
The first is done for you.

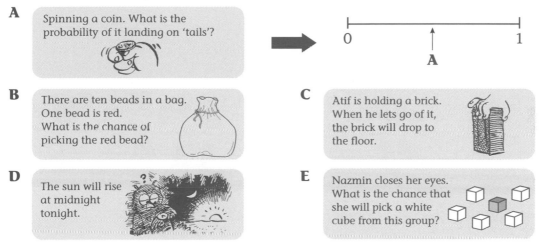

A Spinning a coin. What is the probability of it landing on 'tails'?

0   ↑   1
           A

B There are ten beads in a bag.
One bead is red.
What is the chance of picking the red bead?

C Atif is holding a brick.
When he lets go of it, the brick will drop to the floor.

D The sun will rise at midnight tonight.

E Nazmin closes her eyes.
What is the chance that she will pick a white cube from this group?

Exercise 8

To win, the arrow of the spinner must 'land' on blue.
Match each spinner with one of the probability scales.

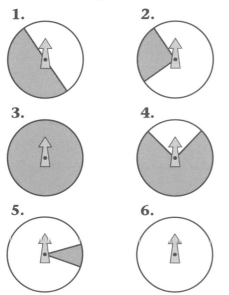

1.   **2.**

3.   **4.**

5.   **6.**

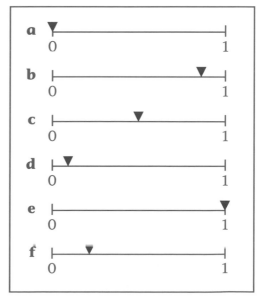

a ▼
      0   1

b   ▼
      0   1

c   ▼
      0   1

d   ▼
      0   1

e   ▼
      0   1

f   ▼
      0   1

14 AVERAGES – MODE, MEDIAN AND MEAN

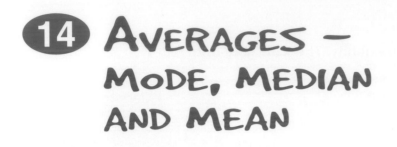

This unit will help you to:
→ **find mode, median, mean**
→ **decide which of these averages is the most useful**
→ **do a simple survey**
→ **collect data and find average values.**

THE MODE

The mode is the most common item in an array.

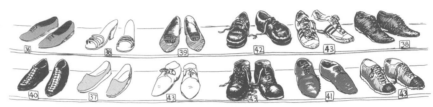

In this array of shoes the most common size is size 43. The **mode** is 43.

Exercise 1

1. What is the modal collar size?

2. What is the modal shoe size?

3. Find the modal temperature from these displays.

Example

In this survey of favourite colours, both blue and red have the same number of votes.
In this case, **both** blue and red are the mode.
You can have more than one mode.

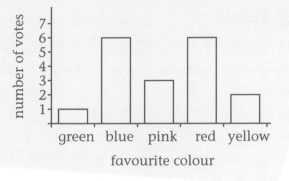

Exercise 2

1. These pie charts show the results of a survey.
   Write down the mode for each of the charts.

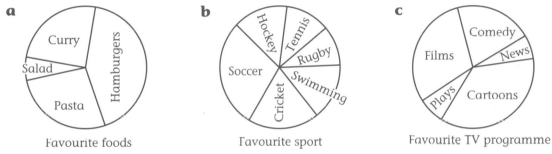

   a Favourite foods   **b** Favourite sport   **c** Favourite TV programme

2. These bar charts display the results of surveys.
   Write down the mode for each display.

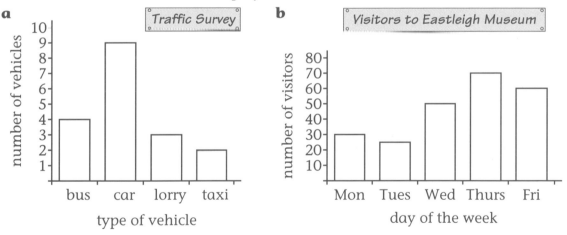

   a Traffic Survey   **b** Visitors to Eastleigh Museum

3. What is the mode for each of these arrays.
   a £5, £3, £11, £7, £11, £8, £3, £7, £11, £8, £9, £11, £6, £7, £8, £12, £8.
   b 16 cm, 22 cm, 12 cm, 16 cm, 12 cm, 23 cm, 14 cm, 12 cm, 15 cm, 19 cm, 16 cm, 12 cm, 22 cm.
   c 11°C, 4°C, 9°C, 16°C, 14°C, 7°C, 9°C, 13°C, 7°C, 11°C, 9°C, 7°C, 13°C, 12°C, 9°C, 8°C, 7°C, 9°C, 18°C, 5°C, 10°C, 10°C, 7°C, 17°C.

4. **a** What is the modal hair colour of your class?
   b What is the modal eye colour of your class?

THE MEDIAN

The median is the middle point in the array.

To find the median you order the array from smallest to largest.

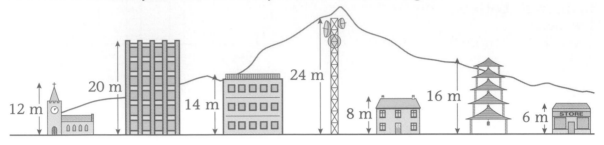

To find the median height of this group of buildings arrange the measurements from smallest to tallest.

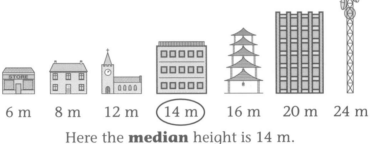

6 m   8 m   12 m   (14 m)   16 m   20 m   24 m

Here the **median** height is 14 m.

Exercise 3

1. Here are a list of temperatures taken at a school at noon each day.
   a Rewrite the temperatures starting with the lowest.
   b Find the midpoint of the array.
      What is the median temperature?

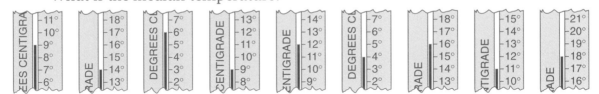

2. A group of students have their height measured.
   What is the median height of this group?

3. The Firebrand basketball team make the following scores during the season.
   What is the median score?

84   110   104   88   98   92   82   66
      96   121   100   71   118

Example

It is easy to find the median if there are an **odd** number of items in an array.

8,   11,   **12**,   14,   15
↑

The median is 12.

When there is an **even** number of items in an array it is more difficult as the midpoint falls between two values.

11,   13,   16,   20,   21,   24
↑
?

To find the median you have to find the midpoint between 16 and 20.

(16 + 20) ÷ 2 = 18

So, the median for this array is 18, because 18 is halfway between 16 and 20.

Exercise 4

1. These numbers have been ordered from smallest to largest.
What is the median for each group?

a 4, 8, 10, 11   **b** 3, 3, 7, 11, 18, 20   **c** 3, 6, 7, 9

2. What is the median height for this group of students?
Start by ordering the list of heights from smallest to largest.

3. Here are the results from an athletics competition.

	100 m sprint	200 m sprint	shot	high jump
Daniel	14.9 sec	32.9 sec	3.35 m	0.78 m
Helder	15.1 sec	34.6 sec	8.85 m	0.68 m
Sarah	14.5 sec	36.8 sec	4.15 m	1.38 m
Taibah	14.7 sec	30.4 sec	8.50 m	0.66 m
Taji	15.3 sec	45.2 sec	7.60 m	1.04 m
David	14.4 sec	34.0 sec	5.20 m	1.22 m
Ergon	16.7 sec	34.4 sec	9.65 m	1.10 m
Lee	15.5 sec	44.2 sec	5.55 m	0.96 m
Ismail	16.6 sec	40.5 sec	8.65 m	1.08 m
Charles	15.4 sec	32.8 sec	7.50 m	0.88 m

a What is the median time for the 100 m sprint?
b What is the median time for the 200 m sprint?
c What is the median distance for the shot?
d What is the median height for the high jump?

THE MEAN

Five friends spend their Saturday morning doing odd jobs in the local market. Their wages are shown below.

We have to think carefully about the average money earned. The **mode** is misleading (**£4**) as most of the group earned more than £4. We could use the **median** (**£7**) but you see that it is not really in the middle of the values. There is another way to give an average, you can use the **mean**. To find the mean:

Add the wages together and divide the total by the number of people in the group:

$$£4 + £4 + £7 + £21 + £24 = £60$$
$$\text{Mean} = \frac{£60}{5} \quad (£60 \div 5)$$
$$= £12$$

Do you think that the **mean** (**£12**) is a better value to use for the **average** wage?

> The mean is the sum of all the values divided by the number of values.

Exercise 5

Find the mean number of items in each group below.

1.

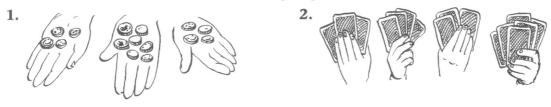

2.

Exercise 6

Calculate the mean amounts of money in each group below.

1. £2, £7, £3, £4
2. £4, £6, £2, £4
3. £10, £32, £2, £4, £7
4. £5, £10, £3, £3, £1, £2
5. £6, £9, £1, £7, £12
6. £24, £17, £49, £30
7. £210, £309, £81
8. £0.15, £2.45, 10p

Exercise 7

Find the missing value in each group.

1. Mean = £5: (£4, £7, £3, £?)
2. Mean = 10 m: (11 m, 13 m, 9 m, ? m)
3. Mean = 9: (14, 15, 6, 2, ?)

Remember
The **mean** is the sum of all the values, divided by the number of values.

Exercise 8

1. The numbers of students that are late to school each morning are recorded over 10 days.

The Head Teacher is asked for the 'average' daily lateness.
She uses the mean as the average. What is the daily average number of late students?

2. The mid-day temperatures over one week in Edinburgh were:

   5°C   7°C   9°C   8°C   6°C   4°C   3°C

What is the average temperature for the week?

3. In her last 6 History tests, Laura scored 19, 23, 28, 28, 23 and 23.
What is Laura's average score?

4. Eddie cycles 8 laps of a cycle track. His times are as follows:

   27 secs   24 secs   21 secs   22 secs   28 secs   34 secs   41 secs   43 secs

What is Eddie's average lap time?

5. The chart below shows the average heights of people from four countries.

Country	Men	Women
Germany	176 cm	164 cm
Japan	166 cm	153 cm
Netherlands	183 cm	170 cm
USA	176 cm	163 cm

a Which country has the tallest people, on average?
b Which country has the shortest people, on average?
c On average, are men taller than women?
d On average, how much taller is a German woman than a Japanese woman?

6. The 'average' (mean) height of basketball players in the NBA is 203 cm.
If you were asked to work out the average height of your class, describe how you would do it.

These are the names and heights of pupils in Class 9W:

Exercise 9

1. Read the scale to find the height of each person.
2. Record the heights in a table like the one opposite.

Table of names and heights of pupils in Class 9W:

Name	Height	Name	Height
Charlotte	1.39 m	Nita	
Chris		Ollie	
Daisy		Peter	
Jerome		Phillipa	
Jane		Ruth	
Joe		Steve	
Lawrence		William	
Lynette			

3. Which are the **modal** heights?
4. Why are these not good values to use as average heights for the class? Think of two reasons why they do not make good averages.
5. Rewrite the list above so that the heights are arranged in order, smallest first. Start: 1.38, 1.39 …
6. Find the **median** value.
7. Add all of the heights together to find the total (it is a good time to use a calculator because there are so many values to add).
8. Divide the total of the heights by the number of pupils.
9. What is the **mean** height of the pupils?
10. Which of the three averages tells you about the typical height of a pupil in Class 9W? Give a reason for your answer.

Exercise 10

1. Repeat Exercise 9 using the shoe sizes of the same class.

   You don't need to do questions 1, 2 or 4.

Name	Shoe size	Name	Shoe size
Charlotte	4	Nita	$2\frac{1}{2}$
Chris	7	Ollie	10
Daisy	2	Peter	5
Jerome	$8\frac{1}{2}$	Phillipa	7
Jane	7	Ruth	4
Joe	3	Steve	7
Lawrence	9	William	3
Lynette	7		

15 STREET MATHS 1: FOOD

This unit will help you to:
→ **improve your mental and written calculations**
→ **understand about kilocalories**
→ **calculate with ratio.**

You eat food to give you energy.
You measure this energy in kilocalories (kcals).

If you eat more kcals than you need, you put on weight.

If you eat less kcals than you need, you lose weight.

An adult needs about 2000 kcals a day.

Jon Minnoch weighed more than 635 kg (100 stones!). When he became unwell, rescuers had to knock down the front door of his home to get him to hospital. They didn't have a stretcher big enough to carry him so they used planks.

Lucin Zarate was the lightest person on record.
At 17 years of age she weighed just over 2 kg.
At 20 years of age she weighed 5.9 kg.

Foods and their Kcal content

Apple	40 kcals	Coffee with milk	30 kcals	Orangeade (can)	110 kcals
Bacon (one slice)	100 kcals	Cola (can)	130 kcals	Peas (30 g)	15 kcals
Baked beans (30 g)	20 kcals	Crisps (bag)	150 kcals	Pizza (small)	305 kcals
Banana	65 kcals	Cocoa (mug)	115 kcals	Potato (boiled)	23 kcals
Beef and kidney pie	525 kcals	Egg (boiled)	80 kcals	Sausage (large)	165 kcals
Bread and butter	40 kcals	Egg (fried)	100 kcals	Sausage roll	290 kcals
Burger (120 g)	430 kcals	Fish finger	55 kcals	Shepherd's pie	500 kcals
Cauliflower (30 g)	3 kcals	Fried fish	330 kcals	Steak pudding	1050 kcals
Chips (per portion)	240 kcals	Lemonade (can)	80 kcals	Sugar (teaspoon)	30 kcals
Chocolate (1 bar)	420 kcals	Milk (250 ml)	150 kcals	Tea with milk	30 kcals

Exercise 1

1. Find the number of kilocalories in each of these four meals.

breakfast   lunch snack   dinner   supper

2. Using the chart above, make up four meals.
Use the chart to add up the number of kcals for each meal.

3. Make up a vegetarian meal.
What is the total number of kcals in it?

When we burn up energy, we use up kilocalories (kcals). All activity uses up kcals. Some activities use up kcals quicker than others.

This list shows how many kcals are used **per minute** (approximately) doing these activities.

Badminton	4	Dancing	5	Lacrosse	6	Swimming	7
Basketball	6	Golf	4	Making beds	7	Tennis	6
Canoeing	5	Hockey	6	Running	13	Walking	5
Cricket	3	Jogging	8	Sleeping	1	Washing up	5
Cycling	6	Judo	7	Soccer	6	Writing	2

Exercise 2

1. How many kilocalories would you use writing for:
   a 8 minutes **b** 10 minutes **c** 15 minutes?
2. How many kilocalories would you use jogging for:
   a 5 minutes **b** 10 minutes **c** 20 minutes?
3. How many kilocalories would you use playing tennis for:
   a 5 minutes **b** 10 minutes **c** 15 minutes?
4. How many kilocalories would you use running for:
   a 3 minutes **b** 5 minutes **c** 10 minutes?

Exercise 3

1. Joe cycles for 10 minutes, then makes his bed in 3 minutes and then sleeps for 20 minutes. How many kilocalories has he used?
2. Jenny plays hockey for 20 minutes, goes running for 5 minutes and then swims for 10 minutes. How many kilocalories has she used?
3. Carlos plays basketball for 10 minutes, jogs for 10 minutes and then plays 10 more minutes of basketball. How many kilocalories has he used?

Exercise 4

Use the table at the top of the page to decide which activity uses up the most kilocalories.

1. Running for 5 minutes **or** dancing for 20 minutes?
2. Washing up for 15 minutes **or** playing badminton for 10 minutes?
3. Playing judo for 20 minutes **or** canoeing for 25 minutes?
4. Sleeping for 1 hour **or** playing cricket for fifteen minutes?

Exercise 5

1.

How many kilocalories does a basketball player use up in the period shown by the clocks?

2.

How many kilocalories would each of two judo players use up during the period shown by the clocks?

3.

How many kilocalories would Fred use sleeping during the period shown on the clocks?

Exercise 6

1. How much do two boxes of mushrooms cost?
2. How much do two bags of celery cost?
3. How much do 2 kg of turnips cost?
4. How much do 3 kg of new potatoes cost?
5. How much do $\frac{1}{2}$ kg of parsnips cost?
6. How much do 4 kg of white potatoes cost?
7. What is the total of each bill?

a
1 kg new potatoes
$\frac{1}{2}$ kg of tomatoes
1 kg of turnips

b
Box of mushrooms
Bag of celery
1 kg carrots

c
$\frac{1}{2}$ kg of peppers
1 kg of sprouts
$\frac{1}{2}$ kg of carrots

Exercise 7

1.

How many boxes of Chilli Chips would you you have to buy to get 120 g?

2.

If you get 6 eggs in a box, how many boxes would you buy to get 42 eggs?

3.

How many biscuits would you get in 5 packets?

4.

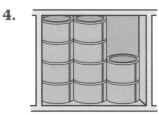

There are 10 cans on this shelf. How many cans would be on a full shelf?

5.

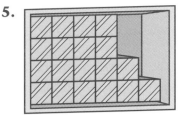

There are 19 boxes on this shelf. How many boxes would be on a full shelf?

6.

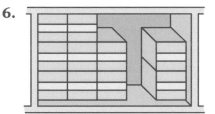

There are 10 packs on this shelf. How many packs would be on a full shelf?

Exercise 8

Which buy do you think is the best value, A or B?

RATIO

Example

To make pastry for pies you need to mix one part of fat with two equal parts of flour.

The ratio of fat to flour is **1 to 2**.
This means that if you used 50 g of fat, you would need 50 g × 2 = 100 g of flour.

Exercise 9

Using the ratio of 1 to 2 for fat to flour, complete the table below.

Parts of fat	Parts of flour
1	2
2	*
4	*
5	*
7	*
3	*
9	*
*	16
*	20
*	80
35	*
42	*

To make butter cream you mix 2 parts of butter with 3 parts of sugar.
This is a ratio of 2 to 3, written as **2 : 3**.

Exercise 10

Using the ratio of butter to sugar as 2 : 3, copy and complete the following problems.
The first is done for you.

1. 4 parts butter : 6 parts sugar

2. 6 parts butter : * parts sugar

3. 8 parts butter : * parts sugar

4. 10 parts butter : * parts sugar

5. 20 parts butter : * parts sugar

6. 40 parts butter : * parts sugar

7. * parts butter : 24 parts sugar

8. * parts butter : 33 parts sugar

Exercise 11

Complete the problems. They are all in the ratio of 3 : 5.
The first one is done for you.

1. 3 : 5 = 6 : 10

2. 3 : 5 = 9 : *

3. 3 : 5 = 18 : *

4. 3 : 5 = 12 : *

5. 3 : 5 = 15 : *

6. 3 : 5 = 30 : *

7. 3 : 5 = * : 35

8. 3 : 5 = * : 50

9. 3 : 5 = * : 500

CookBook

Here are the ingredients Rita used to make herself a mushroom omelette.

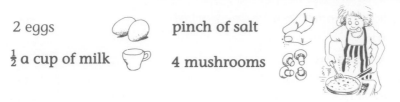

2 eggs   pinch of salt

½ a cup of milk   4 mushrooms

Exercise 12

Write down the ingredients needed for Rita to make omelettes for

a 3 people   **b** 4 people   **c** 10 people

Joe makes a fruit salad for himself. Here are the ingredients that he uses.

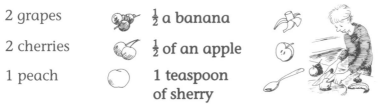

2 grapes   ½ a banana

2 cherries   ½ of an apple

1 peach   1 teaspoon
                  of sherry

Exercise 13

Write down the ingredients needed for Joe to make fruit salad for:

a 4 people   **b** 7 people   **c** 10 people

These are the ingredients to make a chicken curry for 2 people.

½ kg of chicken	4 tablespoons of curry powder
2 potatoes	3 tomatoes
1 tub of yoghurt	250 ml of chicken stock
5 small onions	6 cloves of garlic
50 g of tomato puree	3 cups of rice

Exercise 14

Copy and complete the table below.

Ingredients	For 8 people	For 10 people
Chicken	2 kg	2½ kg
Spoons of curry powder		
Potatoes		
Tomatoes		
Tubs of yoghurt		
Millilitres of chicken stock		
Small onions	20	
Cloves of garlic		
Grams of tomato puree		
Cups of rice		

ꙅ wɘivɘЯREVIEW 2

A. SHAPE

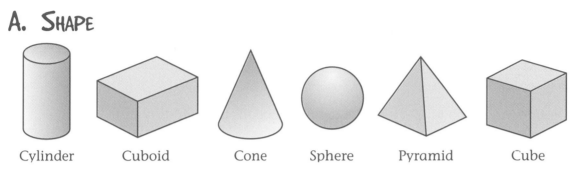

Cylinder   Cuboid   Cone   Sphere   Pyramid   Cube

1. Each of these solids has been put into a sack. By reading the clues, say which solid is in which sack.

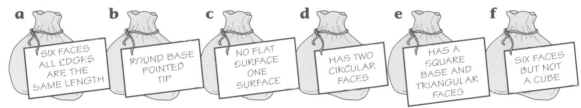

a SIX FACES ALL EDGES ARE THE SAME LENGTH

b ROUND BASE POINTED TIP

c NO FLAT SURFACE ONE SURFACE

d HAS TWO CIRCULAR FACES

e HAS A SQUARE BASE AND TRIANGULAR FACES

f SIX FACES BUT NOT A CUBE

B. VOLUME

What is the volume of these cuboids?

1.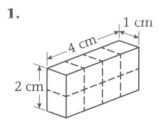

Volume = ___ cm³

2.

Volume = ___ cm³

3.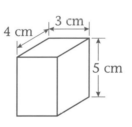

Volume = ___ cm³

What is the length of the missing measurement for each of these rectangular blocks?

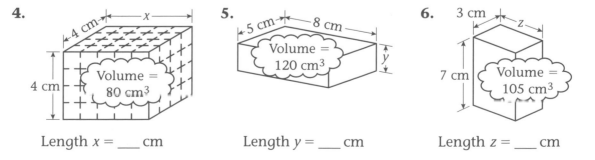

4. 4 cm — x —
4 cm
Volume = 80 cm³

Length x = ___ cm

5. 5 cm — 8 cm —
Volume = 120 cm³
y

Length y = ___ cm

6. 3 cm — z —
7 cm
Volume = 105 cm³

Length z = ___ cm

C. RATIO

1. Which of these drawings shows a ratio boiled eggs to bread soldiers of 2 : 3?

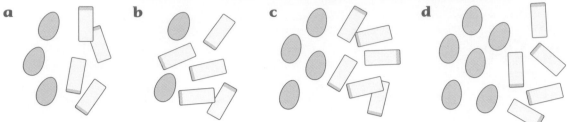

2. Describe the ratio of green beads to orange beads in each drawing.

3. If you need three eggs to make one omelette, how many eggs do you need to make five omelettes?

4. This recipe makes two 'rounds' of shortbread biscuits:

      100 g caster sugar
      200 g butter
      400 g plain flour

  a Rewrite the recipe for one 'round' of shortbread.
  b Rewrite the recipe for four 'rounds' of shortbread.

D. FRACTIONS

1. Louise has £9 and she spent $\frac{1}{3}$ of it. How much did she spend?

2. Find half of these amounts:
  a 18   **b** £12   **c** 24p   **d** 20 cm   **e** £30   **f** 42 kg

3. Find a third of these amounts:
  a 9   **b** 24 kg   **c** 18p   **d** 36   **e** £15   **f** 30 cm

4. What is $\frac{2}{3}$ of 9?

5. What is $\frac{2}{5}$ of 20?

6. What is $\frac{3}{4}$ of 16?

7. What fraction is coloured?

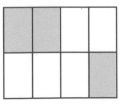

8. What fraction is coloured?

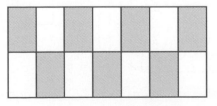

E. AREA

What is the area occupied by these shapes?
They are not drawn full size.

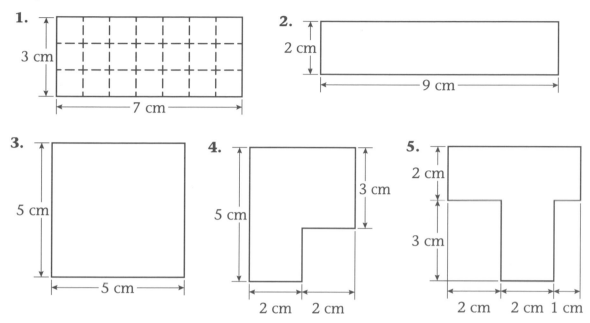

F. ESTIMATION AND ROUNDING OFF

Estimate which answer is the most accurate.

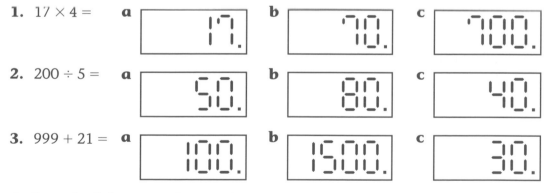

1. $17 \times 4 =$ **a** 17.   **b** 70.   **c** 700.

2. $200 \div 5 =$ **a** 50.   **b** 80.   **c** 40.

3. $999 + 21 =$ **a** 100.   **b** 1500.   **c** 30.

4. Round off these numbers to the nearest ten.

   a 12   **b** 25   **c** 7   **d** 22

   e 51   **f** 69   **g** 34   **h** 56

5. Round off these numbers to the nearest hundred.

   a 140   **b** 99   **c** 250   **d** 730

   e 1290   **f** 460   **g** 310   **h** 892

G. PROBABILITY

There are two aces in each 'hand'. What are your chances of picking the ace?
The first is done for you.
Copy the table and display each probability in three ways:

a in words   **b** as a fraction   **c** on a scale from 0 to 1.

Each hand contains 2 aces	Words	Fraction	Scale
	High probability	$\frac{2}{3}$	0 ——————↑———— 1
			0 ———————————— 1
			0 ———————————— 1
			0 ———————————— 1
			0 ———————————— 1
			0 ———————————— 1

H. ALGEBRA

Find the weight of each parcel.

1.   **2.**   **3.**

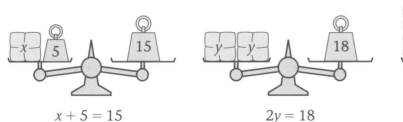

$x + 5 = 15$ $2y = 18$ $2z + 12 = 24 + z$

4. Find the value of the letter in each question.

    a $3b = 9$ **b** $6x = 4x + 2$ **c** $5b = 24 + b$ **d** $30 = 15 + 3q$
    e $2q = q + 5$ **f** $7f = 3f + 16$ **g** $4y = 24$ **h** $33 = 11p$

5. Use the formula $y = 3x + 4$ to find values of y when

    a $x = 1$ **b** $x = 4$ **c** $x = 7$ **d** $x = 20$
    e $x = 5$ **f** $x = 1\frac{1}{2}$ **g** $x = 12$ **h** $x = 2\frac{1}{2}$

6. Alice sells watches in a jewellery shop. She gets a basic wage of £70 a week and a bonus of £2.00 for each watch she sells.

Write a formula to calculate her total wage, using the letter w for total wage and n for the number of watches.

16 STREET MATHS 2: ON THE ROAD

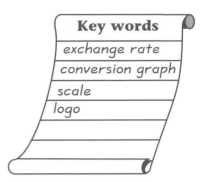

Key words

exchange rate

conversion graph

scale

logo

This unit will help you to:
→ **calculate with large numbers**
→ **use a scale**
→ **use a conversion graph.**

Ray Raver and the Sweet Tones released their new record, 'Keep Cool'.
It sold 13 127 copies during the first week, and entered the Top Ten.

The Top Ten

Group	Title	Sales
The A.K. Band	Rock-set	16 792
T.C. Barret	Jean	11 052
Rupert Groove	Echo, Echo	14 859
The Crew	She's 18	10 237
Crystal Cleer	Wanting You	21 133
The Sweet Tones	Keep Cool	13 127
The Kidz	Warm Nights	13 688
Jail Breakers	Running Back	9 203
The Bio Band	City Sights	11 739
Mitch and Mo	Going West	15 572

Exercise 1

1. Round off the sales figures for each record to the nearest 1 000.
2. Rewrite the Top Ten in order of their sales figures.
   Put the band with the highest sales figures first.
3. How many more records did Crystal Cleer sell than the Sweet Tones?
4. How many records did the top three groups sell altogether?
5. How many groups sold more than 12 000 records?

The Sweet Tones' fan club sends a newsletter to all their fans.
The newsletter contains a profile of each group member.

Ray Raver	Bunny Grey	Leroy LeGrand	Eric Pluto

	Ray Raver		Bunny Grey		Leroy LeGrand		Eric Pluto
Age	33 years	Age	19 years	Age	18 years	Age	27 years
Height	1.83 m	Height	1.56 m	Height	1.91 m	Height	1.66 m
Weight	85 kg	Weight	56 kg	Weight	70 kg	Weight	74 kg
	Lead singer		Keyboards – Saxaphone		Drums		Guitar – Trumpet

Exercise 2

Using the profile above and the clues below answer the question 'Who am I?'

1. I am shorter than Eric. I am ....

2. I weight more than Leroy and less than Ray. I am ....

3. I am the tallest member of the group. I am ....

4. I am heavier than Eric. I am ....

5. I am the third tallest in the group. I am ....

6. I am older than 20, but I don't sing. I am ....

7. I am shorter than 1.70 m and I don't play the guitar. I am ....

8. I weigh more than 72 kg and I don't play the trumpet. I am ....

Exercise 3

Age

1. Ray is ___ years older than Leroy.

2. Eric is ___ years older than Bunny.

3. .... is 14 years younger than Ray.

4. .... is 9 years older than Leroy.

5. Eric is ___ years older than Leroy.

6. The age difference between the oldest and the youngest is ___ years.

Exercise 4

Weight

1. Ray is ___ kg heavier than Eric.

2. Bunny is ___ kg lighter than Ray.

3. Leroy is 15 kg lighter than ....

4. There is 14 kg difference between .... and ....

Exercise 5

Height

1. Leroy is ___ cm taller than Eric.

2. Bunny is ___ cm shorter than Eric.

3. Ray is ___ cm taller than Eric.

4. The height difference between the shortest and the tallest is ___ cm.

Ray Raver and the Sweet Tones begin their first tour of the U.S.A.
They arrive in New York and the first thing they do is exchange
their money for United States dollars($).
They go to a bank and discover that they will get one dollar and
60 cents ($1.60) for each pound.

> For £1 you would receive $1.60
> For £10 you would receive $16
> For £100 you would receive $160

Exercise 6
Each member of the group exchanges some of their English money for dollars. Copy
and complete these sentences.

1. Ray cashes £200, he gets $___ .   **2.** Leroy cashes £300, he gets $___ .

3. Bunny cashes £380, she gets $___ .   **4.** Eric cashes £260, he gets $___ .

Exercise 7
The group go to eat at Jumbo's Burger Bar.
How much do they each spend?

1. Ray's snack	**2.** Leroy's snack	**3.** Eric's snack	**4.** Bunny's snack
= $3·00	= $1·60	= $2·50	= $1·60
= $2·90	= $4·60		= $1·90
= $3·00	= $1·60	= $2·80	
total = $____	total = $____	total = $____	total = $____

Exercise 8
1. The four members of the group went for a bus ride. The fare was $3.60 each.
What was the total cost?
2. The Sweet Tones went to the cinema. The total cost was $46.00. How much did
they each pay?
3. Leroy bought a hamburger for $3.20. He paid for it with a $10 note. How much
change did he get?
4. Bunny bought three magazines. They cost $1.90, $2.60 and $1.85. What was the
total cost?
5. Eric bought two records at $18.95 each. What was the total cost?
6. Ray went out to dinner. His bill came to $31.25. How much change did he get
from $50?
7. The four members of the group each bought a hat. The hats cost $12.75 each.
What was the total cost?

Eric decided that it would be useful to compare the price of things.
He therefore drew up a conversion graph to translate dollars into pounds.

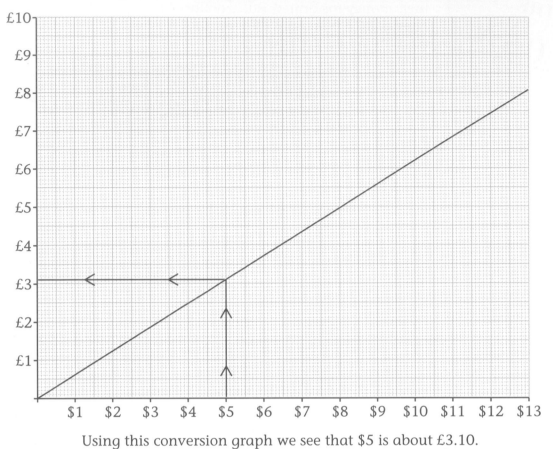

Using this conversion graph we see that $5 is about £3.10.

Exercise 9

Use the conversion graph to find out approximately how much these items cost in pounds and pence.

Exercise 10

Convert these amounts from pounds and pence to dollars and cents.

1. £2.00 is about $___ .   **2.** £5.00 is about $___ .   **3.** £6.00 is about $___ .

4. £1.50 is about $___ .   **5.** £4.50 is about $___ .   **6.** £6.50 is about $___ .

SCALE

Ray Raver and the Sweet Tones are staying in Midchester at the start of their tour.

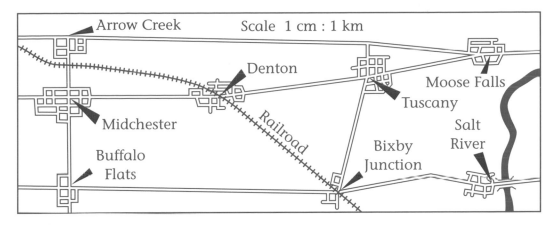

Scale 1 cm : 1 km

Before the concert Ray Raver decided to go for a drive to Denton.
He looked at the map and said, 'It doesn't show how far
Denton is from Midchester'.
'Use the scale', Leroy told him. 'What?' said Ray.

Leroy explains.

'If you measure the distance between Midchester and Denton
on the map, you find they are 4 cm apart. The scale tells you
that each centimetre on the map represents 1 kilometre on the
road'. Midchester is 4 cm from Denton on the map, so Ray will
have to drive 4 km to get from Midchester to Denton.

Exercise 11

Use a ruler to measure the distance between the blue markers.
Convert your answers into kilometres. Remember 1 cm : 1 km.

1. Midchester is ___ km from Buffalo Flats.

2. Midchester is ___ km from Arrow Creek.

3. Tuscany is ___ km from Moose Falls.

4. Tuscany is ___ km from Bixby Junction.

Exercise 12

1. How far is it from Moose Falls to Arrow Creek by the shortest route?

2. How far is it from Buffalo Flats to Salt River by the shortest route?

3. How far is it from Midchester to Moose Falls by the shortest route?

4. If Ray drives from Midchester to Buffalo Flats, Bixby Junction, Tuscany and then
back to Midchester, how many kilometres has he travelled?

5. How far is it from Salt River to Moose Falls by the shortest route?

The Sweet Tones leave Midchester on the next stage of their tour. They go to Austin City.

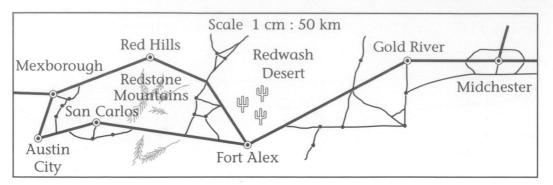

On this map 1 cm represents 50 km. The scale is 1 cm : 50 km.

Exercise 13

The Sweet Tones travel from Midchester to Austin City in their tour coach.

1. The journey from Midchester to Gold River is ___ km.
2. The journey from Gold River to Fort Alex is ___ km.
3. The journey from Fort Alex to San Carlos is ___ km.
4. The journey from San Carlos to Austin City is ___ km.
5. The total journey is ___ km.

Exercise 14

Using the scale above 0.5 cm represents 25 km.

1. How far is it from Austin City to Mexborough by the shortest route?
2. How far is it from Mexborough to Red Hills by the shortest route?
3. How far is it from Red Hills to Fort Alex by the shortest route?
4. How far is it from Gold River to Red Hills by the shortest route?
5. There is a direct air service between Red Hills and Gold River.
   What distance does the aeroplane travel on this journey?

Exercise 15

Redraw this map to scale. Use a scale of 1 cm : 10 km.

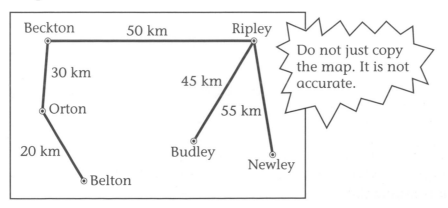

It is the last concert of the Sweet Tones' tour.
5 766 people watch their final performance in the U.S.A.

Exercise 16

1. On which date did most fans attend a Sweet Tones' concert?

2. On which date did least fans attend a Sweet Tones' concert?

3. Rewrite the attendance figures in order, starting with the largest number.

Attendances at concerts	
May 6th	3 424
May 7th	5 834
May 8th	4 616
May 9th	4 209
May 11th	3 974
May 12th	5 282
May 13th	5 575
May 14th	3 121
May 15th	5 065
May 16th	5 766

Exercise 17

1. The cost of a ticket for each concert was $5. How many dollars were received when 3 121 fans came to see the group?

2. The cost of touring was £4 087 for each member of the group. What was the cost for the four of them on tour?

3. The group earned $21 704. How much did each member get?

4. The group travelled 18 808 km by air, 2 698 km by coach, 197 km by train and 64 km by car. How many kilometres did they travel in total?

5. Bunny signed 1 627 autographs, Ray signed 27, Leroy signed 942 and Eric signed 784. How many autographs were signed in total?

6. If 14 songs were sung in 84 minutes, how long on average did each song last?

7. In the middle of their 84 minute act, the group take a 15 minute break. How many hours and minutes does the act last for?

8. During the tour, fans could buy Sweet Tone tee-shirts. 163 blue ones were sold, 198 red shirts, 96 green shirts, and 219 yellow shirts. How many were sold in all?

Returning to Britain the Sweet Tones begin work on their latest record.
The new release is called 'SYMMETRY'.
A cover has to be designed for this new CD.

Exercise 18

The cover of the CD will be $12\frac{1}{2}$ cm by 12 cm.
The design has to be symmetrical.
The name of the band, and the title 'Symmetry' must appear in the design.

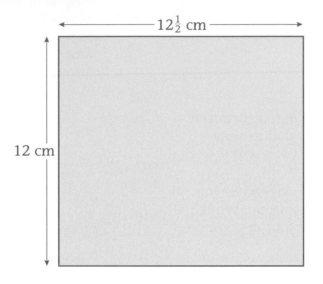

1. The title 'Symmetry' should be in letters 2 cm high.
   a   Draw the shape of the cover, full size.
   b   Draw your symmetrical design.
   c   Make a logo from geometric shapes – the logo should take up $\frac{1}{4}$ of the space.

2. A lapel badge will be given away with each CD.
   The badge has a diameter of 5 cm.
   a   Draw the badge, full size.
   b   Design a logo for the badge.
   c   On the badge print the title 'Symmetry'.

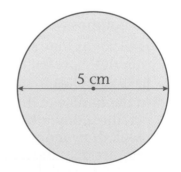

17 AREA AND MULTIPLICATION

Key words

squares
centimetre square
surface area

This unit will help you to:
→ **use your multiplication skill to find the area of squares, rectangles and triangles**
→ **make up your own short cuts to calculate the surface area of simple shapes.**

AREAS

Exercise 1

Peter is tiling his bathroom.
For each drawing say what area has been tiled.

Remember:
Area is measured in **squares**.

1. **2.** **3.**

4. **5.** 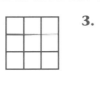 **6.**

Exercise 2

The grey spaces on these drawings show the spaces that have not been tiled yet.
For each drawing   **a**   what area has been tiled
b   what area has not been tiled
c   what is the total area of the wall?

1. **2.** **3.**

4. 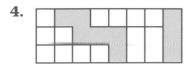 **5.**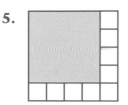

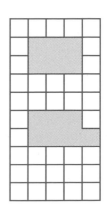

HOW MANY ROWS?

Peter is tiling a wall. There are 9 tiles in each row.
It will take 45 tiles to cover the whole area.
How many rows will he need to make?

If you cannot remember your 9 times table, you can keep subtracting 9 from 45 until you reach 0, or close to it.

$45 - 9 = 36 \dots 1$
$36 - 9 = 27 \dots 2$
$27 - 9 = 18 \dots 3$
$18 - 9 = 9 \dots 4$
$9 - 9 = 0 \dots 5$

I will need 5 rows each with 9 tiles.

Exercise 3

Calculate the number of rows that Peter will tile in each drawing below.

1.

This wall uses 20 tiles and each row has 5 tiles. How many rows will there be?

2.

This wall uses 40 tiles and each row has 8 tiles. How many rows will there be?

3.

This wall uses 40 tiles and each row has 4 tiles. How many rows will there be?

4.

The area of this wall is 60 tiles. There are 15 tiles in each row. How many rows will there be?

5.

The area of this wall is 100 tiles. There are 25 tiles in each row. How many rows will there be?

6.

The area of this wall is 75 tiles. There are 15 tiles in each row. How many rows will there be?

UNITS

The unit for measuring small areas is the **centimetre square**.
This is a centimetre square. Each side is 1 centimetre long.

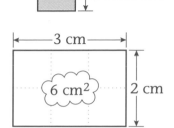

The area of this rectangle is measured by finding how
many centimetre squares (1 cm²) would cover the shape.

Exercise 4

1. Find the area of these shapes by multiplying the **length** by the **width**.
Copy each drawing, and complete the method of giving the answer.

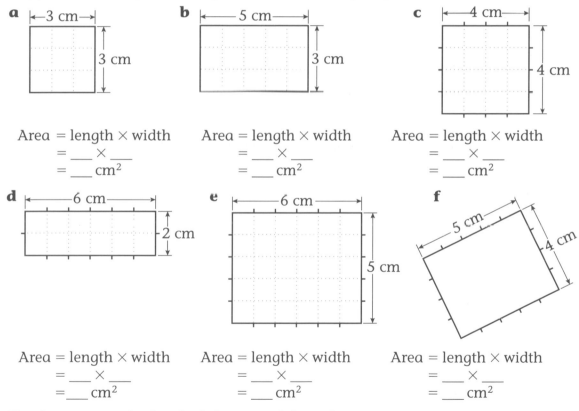

a

Area = length × width
= ___ × ___
= ___ cm²

b

Area = length × width
= ___ × ___
= ___ cm²

c

Area = length × width
= ___ × ___
= ___ cm²

d

Area = length × width
= ___ × ___
= ___ cm²

e

Area = length × width
= ___ × ___
= ___ cm²

f

Area = length × width
= ___ × ___
= ___ cm²

2. Use the same method to find the area of these shapes.

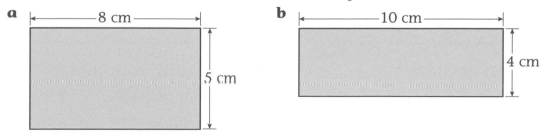

MULTIPLICATION AND AREA

Calculating the area of this rectangle by counting squares would be difficult, because you would have to count 15 squares, 6 times.

$$
\begin{array}{r}
15 \\
15 \\
15 \\
15 \\
15 \\
+\ 15 \\
\hline
90 \text{ cm}^2
\end{array}
$$

15 cm

6 cm

A quicker way is to multiply: $15 \text{ cm} \times 6 \text{ cm}$
Here is one way to do this. You can look back at Unit 6 to remind you of this method.

You can split the rectangle into two smaller shapes:

$$
\begin{array}{r}
10 \times 6 = 60 \text{ cm}^2 \\
+\ \ 5 \times 6 = 30 \text{ cm}^2 \\
\hline
90 \text{ cm}^2
\end{array}
$$

10 cm   5 cm

6 cm

Area = 10×6
= 60 cm^2

Area = 5×6
= 30 cm^2

Exercise 5

Calculate the areas of these rectangles.

The questions have been set out like the example above but if you have your own method, you can use it. **Do not use a calculator**.

1.

16 cm

5 cm | $10 \times 5 = ?$ | $6 \times 5 = ?$

2.

15 cm

8 cm | $10 \times 8 = ?$ | $5 \times 8 = ?$

Area of large rectangle: $10 \times 5 =$ ___

Area of small rectangle: $6 \times 5 =$ ___

Total area   = ___ cm²

Area of large rectangle: $10 \times 8 =$ ___

Area of small rectangle: $5 \times 8 =$ ___

Total area   = ___ cm²

3.

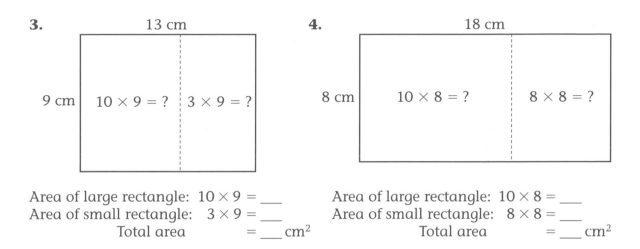

13 cm

9 cm | $10 \times 9 = ?$ | $3 \times 9 = ?$

Area of large rectangle: $10 \times 9 =$ ___
Area of small rectangle: $3 \times 9 =$ ___
          Total area $=$ ___ cm^2

4.

18 cm

8 cm | $10 \times 8 = ?$ | $8 \times 8 = ?$

Area of large rectangle: $10 \times 8 =$ ___
Area of small rectangle: $8 \times 8 =$ ___
          Total area $=$ ___ cm^2

WORKING WITH LARGER NUMBERS

You can use the same method when the sides of the shapes are longer.

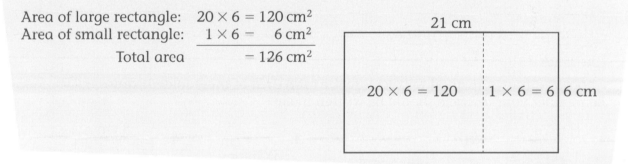

Area of large rectangle: $20 \times 6 = 120$ cm^2
Area of small rectangle: $1 \times 6 = 6$ cm^2
          Total area $= 126$ cm^2

21 cm

$20 \times 6 = 120$ | $1 \times 6 = 6$ | 6 cm

Exercise 6

Calculate the areas of these rectangles without using a calculator.

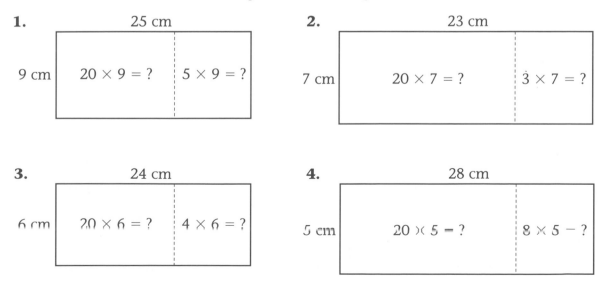

1.

25 cm

9 cm | $20 \times 9 = ?$ | $5 \times 9 = ?$

2.

23 cm

7 cm | $20 \times 7 = ?$ | $3 \times 7 = ?$

3.

24 cm

6 cm | $20 \times 6 = ?$ | $4 \times 6 = ?$

4.

28 cm

5 cm | $20 \times 5 = ?$ | $8 \times 5 = ?$

AREA

This 'Thank You' card has been folded from one piece of card.
The area of the card used can be calculated in two ways:

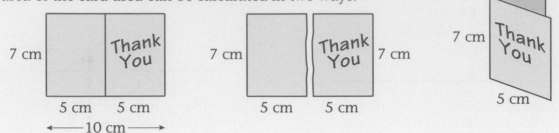

1. Think of the card unfolded into **one piece**. It has a length 10 cm and its width is 7 cm.
   Its area is: 10 cm × 7 cm = 70 cm²

2. Think of the card as **two** smaller cards. The area of each part is:
   5 cm × 7 cm = 35 cm².
   There are two parts so the area of the whole card is: 35 cm² × 2 = 70 cm².

Exercise 7

Choose your own method to calculate the total area of these folded cards.
Remember your answers should be written in cm².

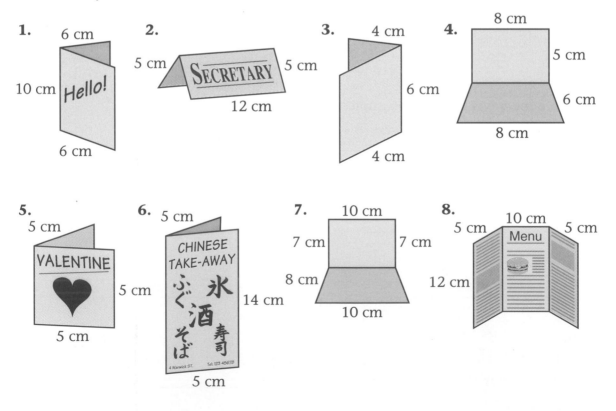

SURFACE AREA

This box has 6 surfaces: This pyramid has 5 surfaces:

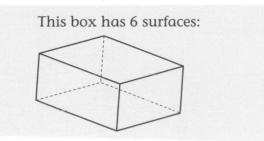

Exercise 8

How many surfaces has each of these shapes?

1.   **2.**   **3.**

4.   **5.**   **6.**   **7.**

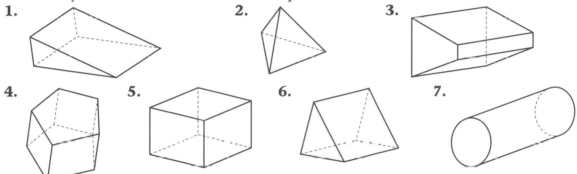

CALCULATING SURFACE AREA

The surface area of this box is the total area of all 6 sides:
$20 \text{ cm}^2 + 20 \text{ cm}^2 + 15 \text{ cm}^2 + 15 \text{ cm}^2 + 12 \text{ cm}^2 + 12 \text{ cm}^2 = 94 \text{ cm}^2$

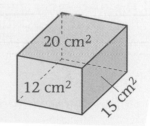

20 cm^2

12 cm^2

15 cm^2

Exercise 9

Calculate the surface area of each shape.

1.   **2.**   **3.**

48 cm^2 24 cm^2 9 cm^2

30 cm^2 20 cm^2 9 cm^2 9 cm^2

40 cm^2 30 cm^2

4.   **5.**   **6.**

24 cm^2 4 cm^2 80 cm^2

16 cm^2 4 cm^2 80 cm^2

6 cm^2 4 cm^2

64 cm^2

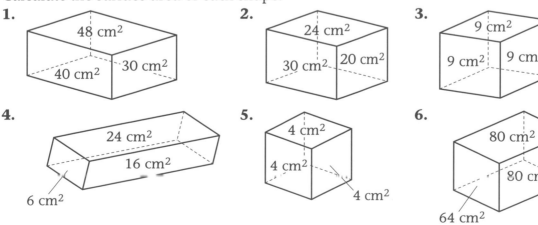

SHORT CUTS FOR FINDING SURFACE AREA

You can see that the faces of the box can
be paired together, because they are congruent,
(exactly the same shape and area):

    top and bottom
    front and back
    left and right sides

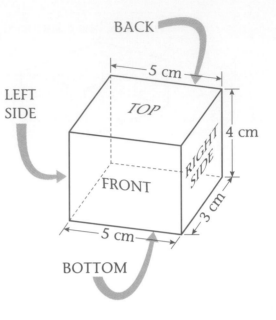

Can you think how this can be used as a
short cut for finding the total surface area?

One way is to find the area of only one of the
pairs of faces then double it.

    area of the top $= 5 \times 3 = 15\,cm^2$
    area of front $= 5 \times 4 = 20\,cm^2$
    area of side $= 4 \times 3 = 12\,cm^2$

Double these because they come in pairs:

    area of top and bottom $= 30\,cm^2$
    area of front and back $= 40\,cm^2$
    area of left and right sides $= 24\,cm^2$

Total surface area $= 30\,cm^2 + 40\,cm^2 + 24\,cm^2$
                    $= 94\,cm^2$

There are other short cuts of your own that you can
find. Swap ideas with your partner.

Exercise 10

Calculate the surface areas of these boxes.

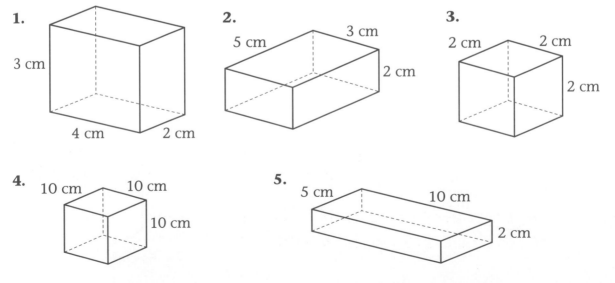

TASK 1

You need: centimetre squared paper
              pencil
              ruler
              scissors

1. Carefully draw a square on to the grid paper. The sides of the square should be 10 cm long.

2. Write down the area of the square.

3. Draw a **diagonal** line, from corner to corner.

4. Carefully cut along the diagonal line.

5. You have made two **triangles**. Fit one on top of the other to check that they have the same **area**.

6. What is the area of each triangle?

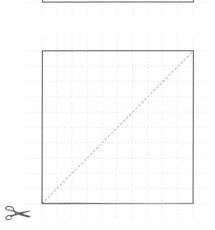

7. Copy and complete this sentence, by thinking about the area of a triangle and the area of the square.
'The area of one of the triangles is .... of the area of the square'.

Exercise 11

What is the area of each of the grey triangles below?

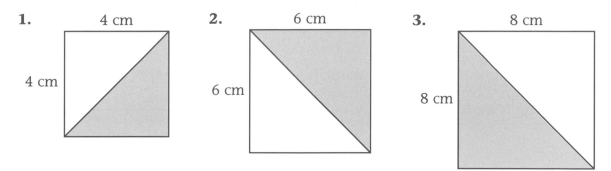

1. 4 cm / 4 cm

2. 6 cm / 6 cm

3. 8 cm / 8 cm

TASK 2

1. Do Task 1 again for a rectangle 8 cm long and 5 cm high.

2. Do you get the same answer to question 7?

Exercise 12

Calculate the areas of these triangles.
Find the area of the rectangle, then halve it to find the area of the triangle.

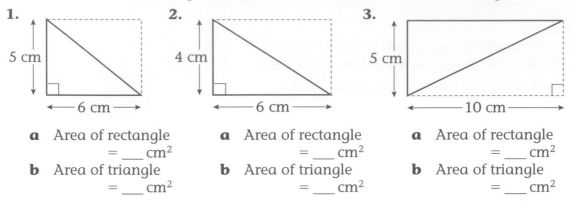

1.   5 cm   6 cm

a   Area of rectangle
      = ___ cm²
b   Area of triangle
      = ___ cm²

2.   4 cm   6 cm

a   Area of rectangle
      = ___ cm²
b   Area of triangle
      = ___ cm²

3.   5 cm   10 cm

a   Area of rectangle
      = ___ cm²
b   Area of triangle
      = ___ cm²

Exercise 13

Calculate the area of these triangles.

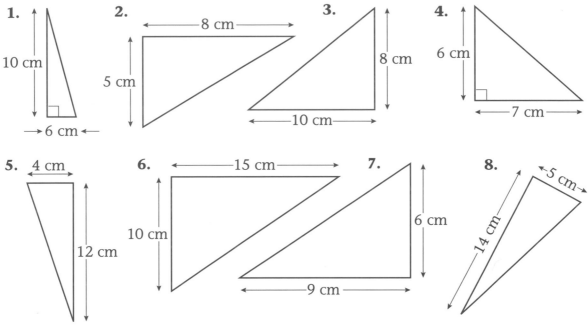

1. 10 cm, 6 cm

2. 8 cm, 5 cm

3. 8 cm, 10 cm

4. 6 cm, 7 cm

5. 4 cm, 12 cm

6. 15 cm, 10 cm, 9 cm

7. 6 cm

8. 5 cm, 14 cm

9. a   Calculate the area of each triangular tile.
    b   What is the area of the whole surface?
    c   What is the total shaded area?

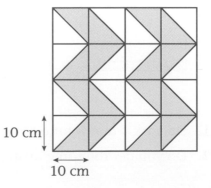

10 cm

10 cm

18 COORDINATES

This unit will help you to:
→ **work with coordinates**
→ **work with patterns on grids**
→ **work with negative numbers.**

The numbered lines are called axes.

This is the *y*-axis

Remember: The first number in a pair of coordinates is on the *x*-axis.
The second number is on the *y*-axis.

This is the *x*-axis

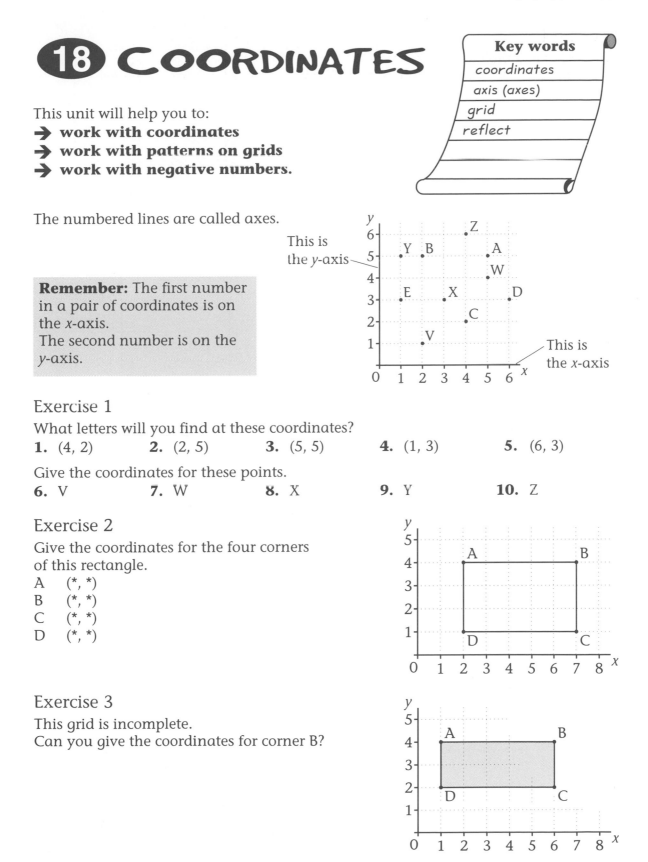

Exercise 1
What letters will you find at these coordinates?
1. (4, 2)　　　**2.** (2, 5)　　　**3.** (5, 5)　　　**4.** (1, 3)　　　**5.** (6, 3)

Give the coordinates for these points.
6. V　　　**7.** W　　　**8.** X　　　**9.** Y　　　**10.** Z

Exercise 2
Give the coordinates for the four corners of this rectangle.
A　(*, *)
B　(*, *)
C　(*, *)
D　(*, *)

Exercise 3
This grid is incomplete.
Can you give the coordinates for corner B?

Exercise 4

This grid is incomplete.
Write down the coordinates for points A, B and C.

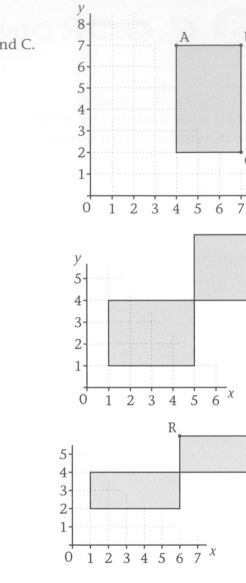

Exercise 5

The rectangles on this grid are identical.
Each rectangle is four units long and three
units high.
What are the coordinates of point Z?

Exercise 6

The rectangles on this grid are identical.
What are the coordinates of points R, S, T?

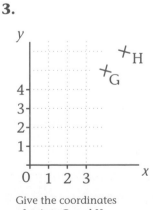

Exercise 7

1.

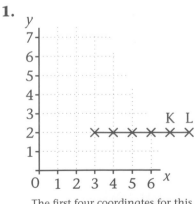

The first four coordinates for this
line are (3, 2) (4, 2) (5, 2) (6, 2)
What are the coordinates of K and L?

2.

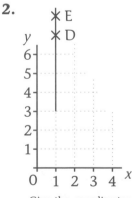

Give the coordinates
of points D and E.

3.

Give the coordinates
of points G and H.

In this diagram the *y*-axis has been extended down below the *x*-axis.

> **Remember:** Numbers used in positions below the *x*-axis have a minus sign in front of them.

The coordinates of point A are (2, ⁻4):
2 along the *x*-axis
⁻4 on the *y*-axis.

Exercise 8

What letter will you find at these coordinates?

1. (4, ⁻2): 4 along the *x*-axis
           ⁻2 on the *y*-axis

2. (2, ⁻3): 2 along the *x*-axis
           ⁻3 on the *y*-axis

3. (5, ⁻5): 5 along the *x*-axis
           ⁻5 on the *y*-axis

Give the coordinates for these points.

4. X   **5.** Y   **6.** Z

In this diagram the *x*-axis has been extended to the **left** of the *y*-axis.

> Numbers in positions to the left of the *y*-axis have a negative sign in front of them.

Point A is at coordinates (2, 3):
2 on the *x*-axis
3 on the *y*-axis

Point B is at coordinates (5, ⁻2):
5 on the *x*-axis
⁻2 on the *y*-axis

Point C is at coordinates (⁻3, 4):
⁻3 on the *x*-axis
4 on the *y*-axis

Point D is at coordinates (⁻4, ⁻3):
⁻4 on the *x*-axis
⁻3 on the *y*-axis

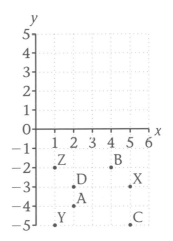

Exercise 9

What letters will you find at these coordinates?

1. (5, 2)   **2.** (4, 5)   **3.** (1, ⁻3)   **4.** (5, ⁻4)

5. (⁻2, 3)   **6.** (⁻4, 2)   **7.** (⁻2, ⁻4)   **8.** (⁻4, ⁻5)

REFLECTION

Example

Look at the grid. The orange rectangle is a mirror image of the white rectangle.

The y-axis acts as a mirror.

Corner A is reflected to corner A_1 (2, 5) → (⁻2, 5)

Corner B is reflected to corner B_1 (4, 5) → (⁻4, 5)

Corner C is reflected to corner C_1 (4, 1) → (⁻4, 1)

Corner D is reflected to corner D_1 (2, 1) → (⁻2, 1)

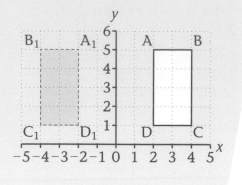

Exercise 10

1. Copy the grid on to centimetre squared paper.
2. Draw the rectangle on the graph and draw its reflection in the y-axis.
3. List the coordinates of the corners of the reflection.

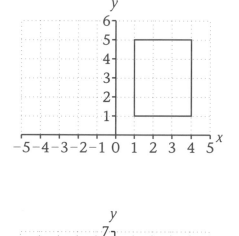

Exercise 11

1. Draw a grid like this on centimetre squared paper.
2. Plot these points on the grid and join them up to form a rectangle:
   (0, 2) (1, 1) (5, 5) (4, 6)
3. Use the y-axis as a mirror to reflect the rectangle.
4. List the coordinates of the reflected rectangle.

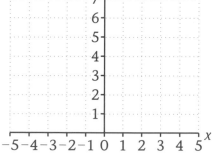

Exercise 12

1. Draw a grid like the one above.
2. Plot these points on the grid: (⁻5, 1) (⁻5, 6) (⁻1, 2).
3. Join up the points to form a triangle.
4. Use the y-axis as a mirror, and list the coordinates of the corners of the reflected triangle.

Example

The grey triangle is the mirror image of the white triangle. The reflection uses the x-axis as the mirror.

Point A is reflected to point A_1 $(4, 2) \rightarrow (4, {}^-2)$
Point B is reflected to point B_1 $(1, 2) \rightarrow (1, {}^-2)$
Point C is reflected to point C_1 $(1, 4) \rightarrow (1, \ 4)$

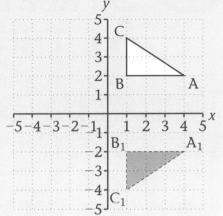

Exercise 13

1. Draw a grid like this one on centimetre squared paper.
2. Draw the shape on the grid.
3. Use the x-axis as a mirror.
4. List the coordinates of A_1, B_1 C_1, D_1, of the reflected shape.

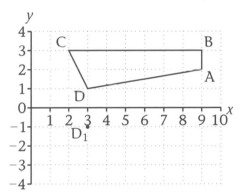

Exercise 14

1. Draw this grid on centimetre squared paper.
2. Draw the shape on the grid.
3. Use the x-axis as a mirror.
4. List all the coordinates of the reflected points A_1, B_1 C_1, D_1, E_1, F_1 G_1, H_1.

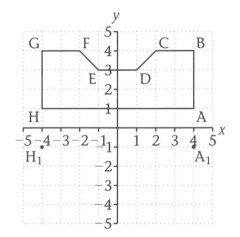

Exercise 15

1. Draw a grid like the one above and plot these points on the grid.
   $({}^-5, 0)$ $({}^-3, 4)$ $(0, 1)$. Join them up to make a triangle.
2. Reflect the triangle in the x-axis and write down the coordinates of the reflected points.

19 STREET MATHS 3: AT THE SHOPS

This unit will help you to:
→ **calculate with money and percentages**
→ **read weighing scales**
→ **understand capacity.**

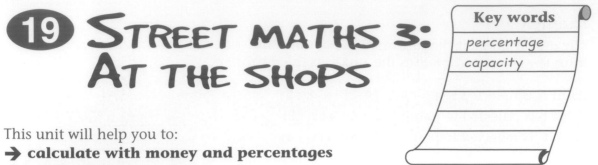

Alex has saved £65 to spend on clothes. He wants to buy a pair of trainers, a pair of trousers and a jumper at the Leisure Wear sale.
Alex decides that these are the items that he likes:

Exercise 1

How much have these items been reduced by?

1. The Ajax trainers
2. The Classic trousers
3. The DeVare jumper
4. The Slimfit trousers
5. The Cobra trainers
6. The Keeval jumper

Exercise 2

1. How much would the **most** expensive pair of trainers, pair of trousers and jumper cost together?
2. How much would the **least** expensive trainers, trousers and jumper cost?
3. Choose a pair of trousers, trainers and jumper that Alex could afford with his £65.
4. Alex bought the Ajax trainers, the Fargo trousers and the Ricco jumper. How much did they cost him?
5. How much change did he have left from his £65?
6. If Alex bought the least expensive trainers, trousers and jumper, how much change would he have left?

PERCENTAGES

In each shop is a sign like this. This sign % means per cent. Per cent means per hundred.

10%

The sign is telling us of a price reduction.

10% means $\frac{10}{100}$ or $\frac{1}{10}$. A 10% reduction means reducing the price by $\frac{1}{10}$.

Exercise 3

These watches are being reduced by 10%. Give the amount of each reduction. The first one has been done for you.

1. 10% of £20 $= \frac{1}{10}$ of £20
$\qquad\qquad\quad = £20 \div 10$
$\qquad\qquad\quad = £2$

2. £50   **3.** £30   **4.** £40   **5.** £10   **6.** £20

7. £70   **8.** £90   **9.** £100   **10.** £110   **11.** £60   **12.** £200

Exercise 4

A 20% reduction means reducing the price by $\frac{2}{10}$ or $\frac{1}{5}$.
If these amounts are all reduced by 20%, give the amount of each reduction.

1. 20% of £10 $= \frac{1}{5}$ of £10
$\qquad\qquad\quad = £10 \div 5$
$\qquad\qquad\quad = £2$

2. £20   **3.** £30   **4.** £60   **5.** £40   **6.** £15   **7.** £25

Exercise 5

A 25% reduction means reducing the price by $\frac{25}{100}$ or $\frac{1}{4}$.
If these amounts are all reduced by 25%
a find the reduction   **b** find the new price.
1. £40   **2.** £16   **3.** £20   **4.** £24   **5.** £80   **6.** £32

Example

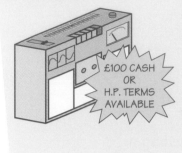

£100 CASH OR H.P. TERMS AVAILABLE

Carol wants to buy a cassette player. She can buy it with cash or buy it by paying fixed instalments over a period of time (hire purchase).
The cost of the machine is £100 cash
                    or
20% of the cost as a deposit, and £10 a month for 10 months.

Deposit   20% of £100   = £20
Instalments £10 × 10 months = £100
                Total cost   = £120

It is therefore £20 dearer to buy this machine on hire purchase.

Exercise 6

Carol wishes to buy this machine which costs £50 cash.
The hire purchase arrangements are:
        10% deposit and £10 a month for 5 months.

1. Copy and complete these calculations to find the cost of payment by hire purchase.
Deposit   10% of £50   = *
Instalments £10 × 5 months = *
            Total cost   = *

2. How much more does it cost to buy the cassette player on hire purchase?

Tommy wishes to buy this television costing £200 cash.
The hire purchase arrangements are:
        20% deposit and £20 a month for 12 months.

3. Copy and complete these calculations to find the cost of payment by hire purchase.
Deposit   20% of £200   = *
Instalments £20 × 12 months = *
            Total cost   = *

4. How much more does it cost to buy the television by hire purchase?

Mrs Lewis wishes to buy this freezer costing £150 cash.
The hire purchase arrangements are:
        10% deposit and £15 a month for 12 months.

5. What is the total cost of buying the freezer by hire purchase?

6. How much more does it cost to buy the freezer by hire purchase?

Marco and Jean are shopping in the market.
They are buying fruit and vegetables.

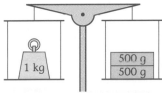
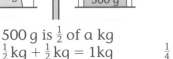

Exercise 7

How much will Marco and Jean pay for:

1. two kilograms of cabbage
2. two kilograms of tomatoes
3. two kilograms of apples
4. three kilograms of potatoes
5. three kilograms of oranges
6. three kilograms of carrots?

There are 1000 grams in a kilogram.

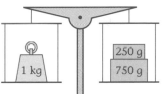

500 g is $\frac{1}{2}$ of a kg
$\frac{1}{2}$ kg + $\frac{1}{2}$ kg = 1kg

250 g is $\frac{1}{4}$ of a kg
$\frac{1}{4}$ kg + $\frac{1}{4}$ kg + $\frac{1}{4}$ kg + $\frac{1}{4}$ kg = 1kg

750 g is $\frac{3}{4}$ of a kg
$\frac{3}{4}$ kg + $\frac{1}{4}$ kg = 1kg

Exercise 8

How much will Marco and Jean pay for:

1. 500 g of oranges
2. 500 g of tomatoes
3. 500 g of pears
4. 500 g of apples
5. 500 g of peas
6. 500 g of carrots?

Exercise 9

How much will Marco and Jean pay for:

1. 250 g of potatoes
2. 250 g of cabbage
3. 250 g of peas
4. 750 g of pears
5. 750 g of potatoes
6. 750 g of cabbage?

Exercise 10

What weights are being used to balance these scales?

1.
2.
3.

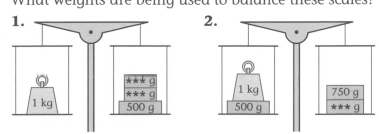
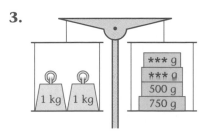

Exercise 11

Every year at Christmas, Mr Farr sends sweets to the children's ward of the local hospital.

1. How many kg of sweets did he send to the hospital if he packaged up:

>   450 g of nut crunch
>   800 g of chocolate fudge
>   600 g of bitter fruit drops
>   750 g of assorted toffees
>   350 g of cola cubes
>   500 g of chocolate buttons

2. Mr Farr sends some sweets to the local junior school. How many kilograms did he send if he packed up:

>   250 g of chocolate eclairs
>   550 g of strawberry chews
>   300 g of bitter lemons
>   200 g of chocolate limes
>   450 g of liquorice allsorts

3. Mr Farr has to reorder stock.
    Here is his order form.
    How many kilograms of sweets is he ordering?

ORDER FORM
FROM: Farr's Sweetshop   TO: Sweet Supplies

Toffee Cubes	1.50 kg	Cola Cubes	1.50 kg
Chocolate Limes	1.75 kg	Butter Lemons	1.25 kg
Nut Crunch	2.25 kg	Nut Toffees	1.50 kg
Choc-mints	1.00 kg	Fizzy Chews	2.50 kg

Exercise 12

What weight will be shown on these scales?

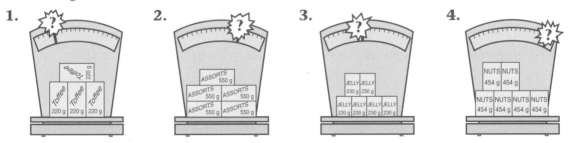

1.   2.   3.   4.

How many grams does each pack weigh?

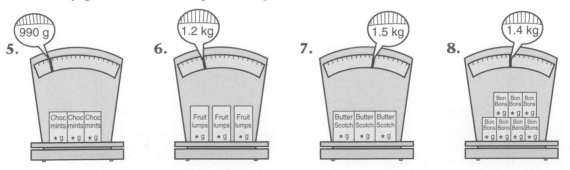

5. 990 g   6. 1.2 kg   7. 1.5 kg   8. 1.4 kg

CAPACITY

Capacity is a measure of volume. When you buy liquids like petrol, wine, or lemonade the amount that you buy is measured in litres (ℓ).

A litre is just a little less liquid than 2 pints.

For measuring small amounts of liquid we can use millilitres (mℓ).
There are 1000 millilitres in a litre.

1 litre = 1000 mℓ.
$\frac{1}{2} \ell = 0.5 \ell = 500 \, m\ell$
$\frac{1}{4} \ell = 0.25 \ell = 250 \, m\ell$
$\frac{3}{4} \ell = 0.75 \ell = 750 \, m\ell$

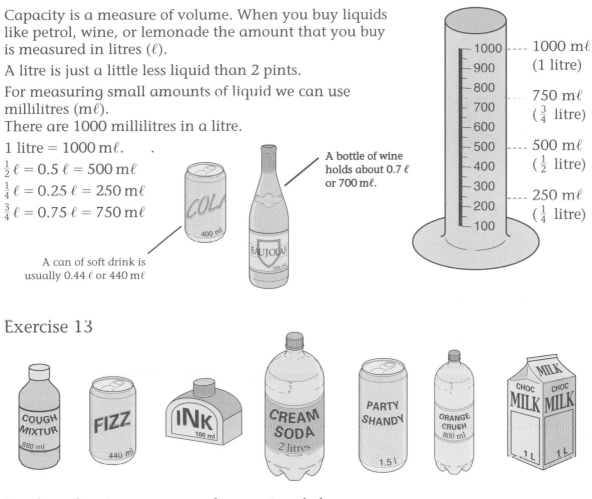

A bottle of wine holds about 0.7 ℓ or 700 mℓ.

A can of soft drink is usually 0.44 ℓ or 440 mℓ

1000 ---- 1000 mℓ
(1 litre)

750 mℓ
($\frac{3}{4}$ litre)

500 mℓ
($\frac{1}{2}$ litre)

250 mℓ
($\frac{1}{4}$ litre)

Exercise 13

Use these drawings to answer the questions below.

Say whether these statements are true or false.

1. 1 bottle of cough mixture is less than 1 ℓ.

2. 1 bottle of ink is more than 250 mℓ.

3. There is more liquid in the Orange Crush bottle than there is in the bottle of cough mixture.

4. One bottle of Cream Soda contains the same amount of liquid as two cartons of Choc Milk.

5. A can of Fizz and a can of Shandy together contain more liquid than a bottle of Cream Soda.

6. The capacity of two cans of Fizz is the same as one bottle of cough mixture.

7. It would take exactly twenty bottles of ink to fill 1 Cream Soda bottle.

8. The contents of a can of Shandy will fit into an empty Choc Milk carton.

THE CASE OF THE MISSING 2P

Tony goes to the sweet shop and encounters a strange problem.

Tony, Bob, Ann and Jenny are out walking. They decide to buy some sweets.

Bob, Ann and Jenny each have 10p, but Tony has no money.

The three of them agree that if Tony goes to get the sweets, they will give him some.

Tony goes to the shop and spends 26p on Chew Drops. He gets 4p change and runs back to his friends

When he returns with the sweets and the 4p change, he gives each of his friends back one penny and they tell him to keep one penny for himself . . . but

Tony gave his friends one penny each, which meant they each paid 9p.

9p + 9p + 9p = 27p

Tony has 1p, which makes 28p.

Since he started with 30p, where is the other 2p?

20 GRAPH SKILLS

Key words
protractor
mode/modal
sections

This unit will help you to:
→ **understand and read different types of graph**
→ **improve your graphical skills**
→ **read and draw pie charts.**

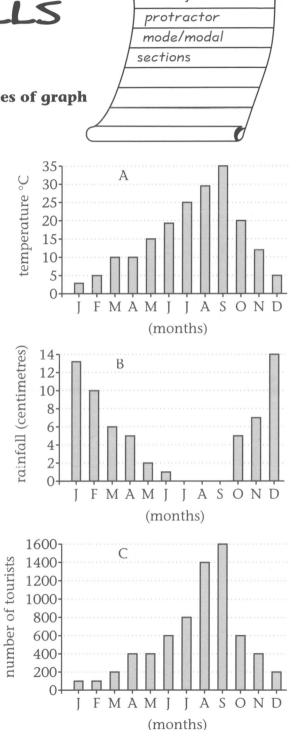

Exercise 1

Graph A shows the average monthly temperature.
1. Which was the hottest month?
2. Which was the coolest month?
3. What was the average temperature in May?

Exercise 2

Graph B shows the average monthly rainfall.
1. Which were the driest months?
2. Which was the wettest month?
3. In which month did 7 cm of rain fall?

Exercise 3

Graph C shows the average number of tourists.
1. In which month did most tourists visit?
2. In which months did least tourists visit?
3. In which month were there 800 visitors?

Exercise 4

Use all the graphs to answer these questions.
1. In which month did 400 tourists visit, and 2 cm of rain fall?
2. Why do you think so many tourists left between September and October?
3. How many visitors came during the three coolest months?

SEISMOGRAPH

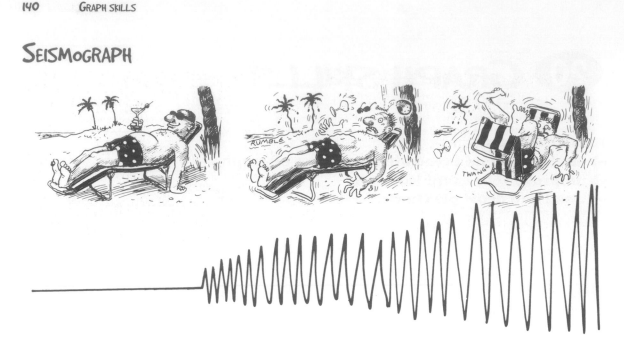

The Seashell Islands suffer from earth tremors. These tremors are measured on a SEISMOGRAPH. When the ground shakes it rocks a pen on a moving sheet of paper. The more violent the tremor the more violently the pen rocks.

Here is a seismograph record for 8 days.

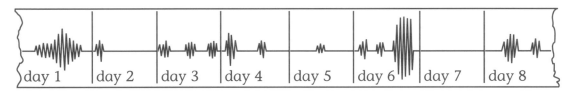

| day 1 | day 2 | day 3 | day 4 | day 5 | day 6 | day 7 | day 8 |

Exercise 5

1. How many tremors were there on day 4?
2. How many tremors were there on day 3?
3. On which day were there no tremors?
4. Which day had the tremor lasting the longest time?
5. Which day had the most violent tremors?

Exercise 6

Here is a graph of earth tremor activity on day 1.

Using the seismograph record above draw a graph for each of the other days.

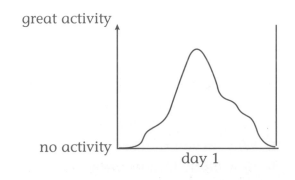

great activity

no activity

day 1

OTHER GRAPHS

Stage 1   Stage 2   Stage 3

This graph shows how brightly the firework burns from the moment it is lit.

Stage 1. It starts off dull becoming brighter.

Stage 2. it burns very brightly for a while.

Stage 3. It burns out and becomes dark again.

Exercise 7
Match the graphs with the correct statements below.

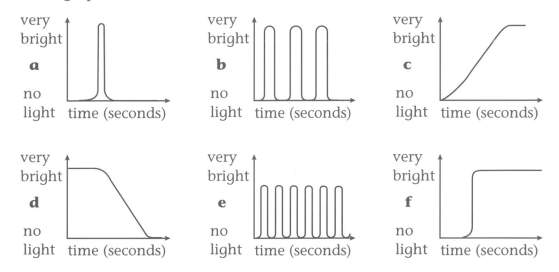

1. Car headlights flashing three times.
2. A light is switched on quickly in a dark room.

3. A flash light flashes once.
4. Cinema lights being dimmed slowly.

5. A car indicator flashing many times.
6. Cinema lights being brightened slowly.

Exercise 8

Match the sentences below with the correct temperature graph.
For example, sentence **a** matches with graph **1**.

a   The temperature starts from 0°C and climbs steadily.

b   The temperature falls steadily from 20°C to 0°C.

c   The temperature rises and falls very quickly.

d   The temperature rises, stays the same for a while and climbs again.

e   The temperature stays the same at 0°C, then rises.

f   The temperature stays the same throughout.

g   The temperature stays the same then falls steadily.

h   The temperature rises, stays warm and then falls steadily.

i   The temperature starts above 0°C and increases steadily.

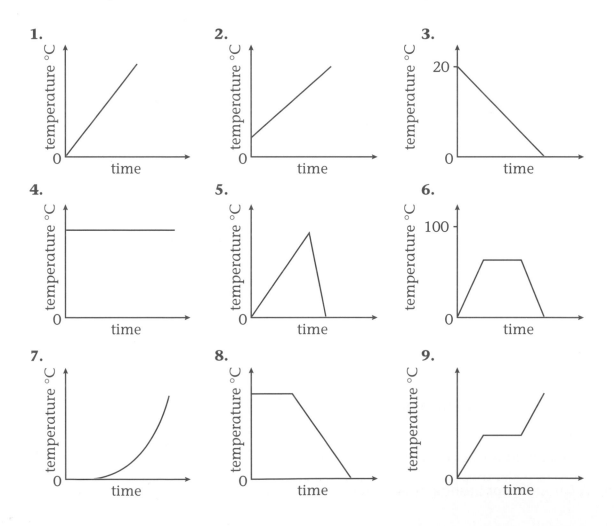

ACTIVITY GRAPH

The graph shows how active Linda was during a full day on holiday at Pontlins Holiday Camp.

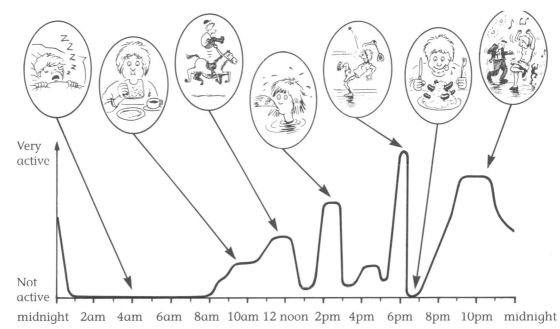

Exercise 9

1. For approximately how long was Linda asleep?

2. At approximately what time did Linda go to bed?

3. Was the build up of activity to horse riding gradual or sudden?

4. What is Linda doing when she is most active?

5. Which activity, other than sleeping, did Linda spend the longest doing?

6. Between horse riding and swimming was Linda resting or busy?

Exercise 10

On axes like the ones below draw an activity graph for your own school day.

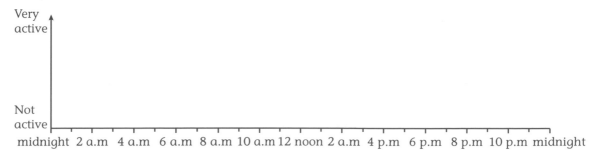

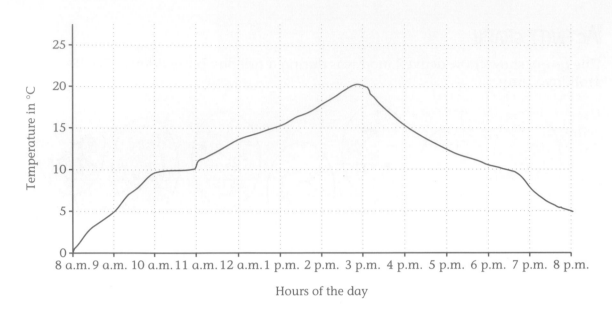

Hours of the day

Exercise 11

Answer these questions about the graph above.

1. Is the temperature rising or falling between 8a.m. and 3p.m?
2. What is happening to the temperature between 3p.m. and 7p.m?
3. What is happening to the temperature between 10a.m. and 11a.m? Is it
    a rising
    b staying constant
    c falling?
4. At what times did the temperature reach 15°C?
5. When did the temperature reach its highest?
6. What was the highest temperature reached?

Exercise 12

Answer these questions about the graph below.

1. What was the temperature at 6a.m?
2. What was approximately the highest temperature reached?
3. What was approximately the lowest temperature reached?
4. About what time did the temperature reach its highest?
5. About what time did the temperature reach its lowest?
6. Did the temperature fall quicker than it rose?

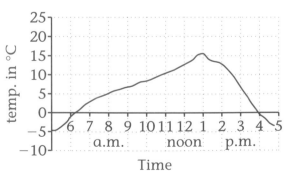

Time

PIE GRAPHS

This **pie graph** shows the results of a survey of favourite break time snacks in two Year 9 classes.

The pie graph does not show a lot of detail, but it lets you see the 'picture' or the trends, quickly.

It is easy to see that the most popular choice is sweets. This is the **mode**.

It is also easy to see that the next popular choice is crisps and that filled rolls and soup are equal choices.

Favourite break time snacks in Year 9

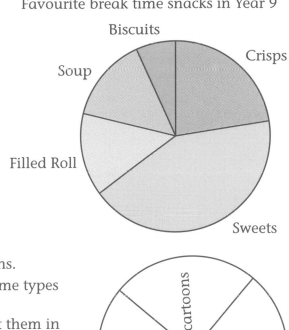

Exercise 13

Read the pie graph to answer these questions.

1. How many different television programme types were chosen by the students?

2. Make a list of the programme types. Put them in order from the least to the most popular.

3. **a** Which is the **modal** programme choice?
   b Explain how you decided on your answer?

4. **a** Cartoons and comedy programmes had the same number of votes. Can you tell from the graph how many votes each type of programme received?
   b What **fraction** of the votes did they receive between them?

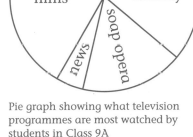

Pie graph showing what television programmes are most watched by students in Class 9A

TASK 1   Making a sketch of a pie graph

1. Either **a** collect information about your class's favourite types of television programmes
   or   **b** imagine what you think your class friends would choose as their favourite programmes.

2. Use a pair of compasses to draw a circle. Mark the centre of the circle clearly with a fine dot.

3. Use the data that you collected or that you imagined, to **sketch** a pie graph of favourite television programmes.

4. How did you estimate how big the sections of the circles had to be?

5. How could you make the chart more accurate?

TASK 2 DRAWING AN ACCURATE PIE GRAPH

The data, or information, on the frequency table was collected by Class 9A. It tells you about the animals kept as pets by some Year 9 students.

1. Copy the frequency table. Use the tally to fill in the frequency column. (Leave the angle column until later.)

Animal	Tally	Frequency	Angle
Dog	|||| |||| ||		
Bird	||||		
Fish	|||	3	$3 \times 10 = 30°$
Cat	|||| ||||		
Hamster	|||| |	6	$6 \times 10 = 60°$
	Total		360°

2. Calculate the total number of choices made, by adding up the frequency column. (The frequency total should be 36.)

Calculating the angles for each section of the pie graph.

You should have worked out that the total number of 'choices' is 36.

So imagine that the pie graph has 36 equal pieces.

Since the pie graph is a circle, the 36 pieces take up 360°.

Each of the pieces would take up: $360° \div 36 = 10°$

Each piece is 10°

3. Go back to the table and fill in the angle needed for each pet's section of the pie graph, like this:

hamster, 6 choices: $6 \times 10° = 60°$

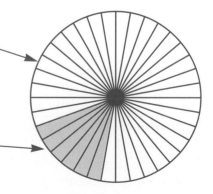

Drawing the pie graph

4. Draw a circle with a radius of 12 cm.

5. Mark the centre of the circle with a clear but fine dot.

6. Draw a fine radius line.

7. Measure and draw the first angle from the table: 120°.

8. Label this section 'Dog'.

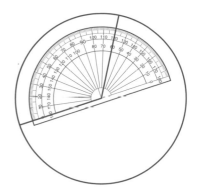

9. Turn your protractor around as this drawing shows.

10. Draw the next angle from the table: 50°.

11. Label this section 'Bird'.

12. Continue like this until you have completed all five sections.

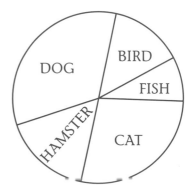

The finished drawing will look like this.

Questions to think about

a What will happen if you draw the circle very small?

b Does it matter where you draw the first radius line?

c Do you have to draw the sections in a special order?

d Can you write the angles on to each section of the pie graph?

Exercise 14

Follow the steps on the previous page to draw pie charts for each of these frequency tables below.

a Copy each table.

b Find the number of equal pieces needed for each pie graph (total number of 'choices').

c Find the angle of each piece (360° ÷ number of pieces).

d Calculate the angle of the section for each choice.

e Draw the circle. Use a protractor to finish the pie graph.

f Label each part of the graph and give the graph a title.

1. Frequency table showing choices of best liked sandwich fillings.

Filling	Frequency	Angle
salad	1	
tuna	4	
cheese	3	
chicken	2	
total		360°

2. Frequency table showing how Year 9 students like to spend their free time.

Pastime	Tally	Frequency	Angle
shopping	IIII IIII IIII		
surfing the net	IIII IIII IIII IIII		
playing computer games	IIII IIII		
doing maths homework	IIII IIII IIII		
athletics	IIII IIII IIII IIII IIII IIII		
Total			360°

Exercise 15

Make a small survey of your own.

a Decide what information your survey will find out.

b Collect the data and put it on to a frequency table like the ones above.

c Draw a pie graph to display the data.

Ǝ WƎIVƎᴚ REVIEW 3

A. SYMMETRY

1. Look at these painted eggs. Which of them are drawn symmetrically?

a   **b**   **c**   **d**   **e**

2. Copy these shapes. Draw the lines of symmetry on them.

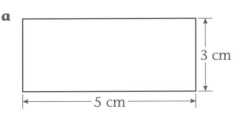

a

3 cm

5 cm

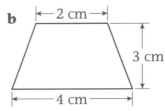

b   ⟵ 2 cm ⟶

3 cm

4 cm

B. PROBLEMS

1.

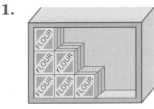

a How many bags of flour are in this box?

b How many bags would be in a full box?

2.

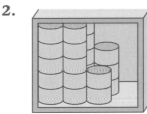

a How many tins are in this box?

b How many tins would be in a full box?

Complete these problems so that they are correct.

3. a
```
    2 3 *
  + 1 * 2
  -------
    3 8 6
```
b
```
    3 * 5
  + 3 4 *
  -------
    6 7 9
```
c
```
    4 5 8
  + 2 * *
  -------
    6 8 2
```
d
```
    * 6 *
  + 4 * 7
  -------
    6 9 3
```

e
```
    6 8 5
  - 3 * *
  -------
    3 6 1
```
f
```
    5 * 7
  - 3 3 *
  -------
    2 5 4
```
g
```
    6 * 9
  - * 5 3
  -------
    4 2 *
```
h
```
    7 6 0
  - 3 * *
  -------
    4 4 4
```

i
```
  2 3 ×
      *
  -----
  4 6
```
j
```
  3 * ×
    2
  -----
  6 8
```
k
```
  2 * ×
    3
  -----
  6 9
```
l
```
  2 * * ×
      3
  -------
  6 9 6
```

m
```
    2 3
  * )6 9
```
n
```
    4 3
  2 )8 *
```
o
```
    2 4
  2 )* *
```
p
```
    * 0 4
  3 )6 1 *
```

C. ANGLES IN A CIRCLE

What would the tank be aiming at if the barrel pointed at these bearings?
(Use a ruler to help you.)

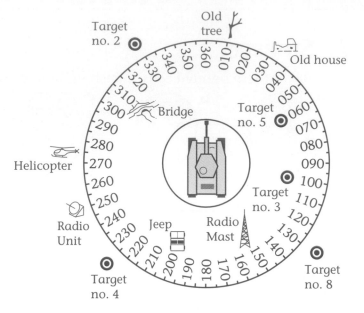

1. 060°

2. 130°

3. 250°

4. 010°

5. 310°

What are the bearings for these targets?

6. The Radio Unit

7. Target No. 3

8. Target No. 2

9. The Old House

10. The Helicopter

11. How many degrees of turn are there between the Old Tree and Target No. 5?

12. How many degrees of turn are there between the Old House and Target No. 3?

13. How many degrees of turn are there between Target No. 8 and the Jeep?

14. How many degrees of turn are there between the Helicopter and Target No. 2?

15. How many degrees of turn are there between the Radio Unit and the Old House?

D. AVERAGES

The **median** is the middle value in an array.

The **mode** is the most common value in an array.

The **mean** is the total of all the values divided by the number of values.

1. Find the median value in this group of test results.
   60, 43, 47, 61, 35, 53, 49, 32, 59

2. Find the mode of this array of shoe sizes.
   43, 41, 39, 39, 41, 37, 39, 35, 45

3. Find the mean for this array of scores.
   6, 7, 6, 8, 8

4. Find the mean for these amounts of money.
   20p, 10p, 12p, 8p, 15p, 1p

E. COORDINATES

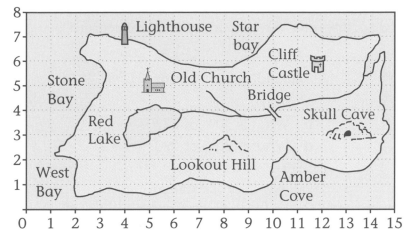

Rewrite this passage replacing two coordinates with place names from the map.

They landed at (2, 2) and went to (4, 3) where they stopped to drink. From (4, 3) they made their way to (8, 3). From the summit they could see (12, 6) and the (4, 7). They left (8, 3) and walked to (13, 3) where they had lunch. On the way back to (2, 2) they crossed a (10, 4) and passed by an (5, 5).

F. SOLIDS

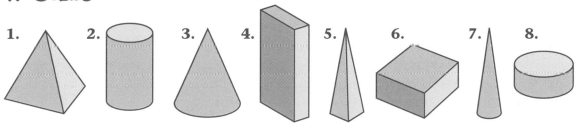

These solids have been re-drawn below. The views have been changed.
Copy the table, then match the solids and name them.
The first has been done for you.

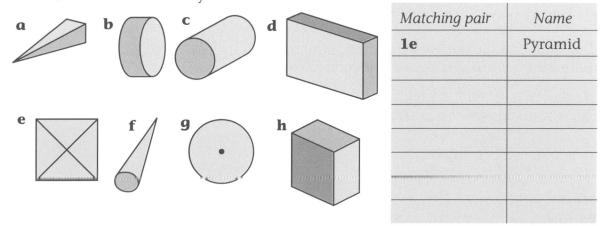

Matching pair	Name
1e	Pyramid

G. PERCENTAGES

A 30% reduction means reducing the price by $\frac{3}{10}$.
If these amounts are all reduced by 30%, give the amount of each reduction.

1. £10
2. 50p
3. £2.50
4. 20p

5. £700
6. £60
7. £40
8. £1.50

9. Answer the following questions.
   a What is 10% of £40?
   b What is 50% of £220?
   c What is 25% of £50?
   d What is 20% of £90?

H. REFLECTIONS

1. a Copy the grid and draw the triangle ABC on to the grid.
   b Use the *y*-axis as a mirror, and draw the reflection of the triangle.
   c Write down the coordinates of the reflection, $A_1 B_1 C_1$.

2. a Copy the grid and draw the shape ABCD on to the grid.
   b Use the *x*-axis as a mirror and draw the reflection. Write down the coordinates of the reflected shape ($A_1B_1C_1D_1$).

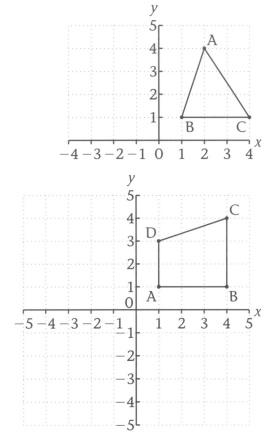

I. DECIMALS

Copy and find the answers to the following calculations.
(Estimate your answers before you do your calculations.)

1. 5.2 kg + 9.7 kg − 3.8 kg = *
2. 8 kg − 7.2 kg = *
3. 3.2 m + 4.9 m + 10 m = *
4. 0.2 m + 1.5 m + 1.3 m = *
5. 3.5 m − 1.20 m = *
6. 9.1 m + 10.5 m − 13 m = *
7. 4.2 × 4 = *
8. 3.1 × 3 = *
9. 5.2 × 4 = *
10. 6.2 × 3 = *
11. 2.5 × 3 = *
12. 0.9 × 2 = *
13. 16.3 × 3 = *
14. 15.6 × 4 = *
15. 4.8 ÷ 2 = *
16. 3.9 ÷ 3 = *
17. 15.3 ÷ 3 = *
18. 2.7 ÷ 9 = *

J. PROBABILITY

Answer these questions.

1. When tossing a coin, what is the probability of it being a 'head'?

2. What is the probability of getting a 'tail'?

For the questions below, use a dice or a picture of a dice to help you.

3. What is the probability of rolling a 'four'?

4. What is the probability of rolling a 'six'?

5. What is the chance of rolling a 'two' or a 'one'?

6. What is the chance of rolling a 'three' or a 'six'?

7. What is the probability of rolling a 'one', a 'two' or a 'three'?

8. What is the probability of rolling a number bigger than 'four'?

K. GRAPHS

This graph shows the number of hours the sun shone on different days in a week.

1. On which day did the sun shine longest?

2. On which day did the sun shine for 3 hours?

3. For how long did the sun shine on Sunday?

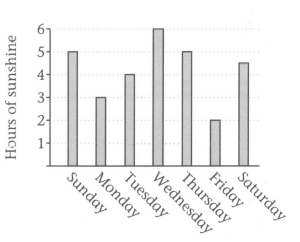

4. Below are three graphs. Match each graph with the statement that describes it.

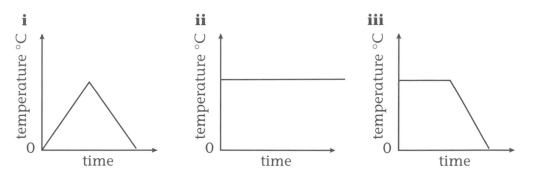

i   **ii**   **iii**

a The temperature stays constant throughout.

b The temperature rises steadily then falls steadily.

c The temperature is constant, then falls steadily.

L. CHOOSING THE RIGHT UNITS

The events in the drawings below involve **time**, **money**, **distance and length**, **volume**, **temperature**, **weight** and **speed**.

Look at these statements.

Which statement goes with which drawing?